# Choirs of Angels

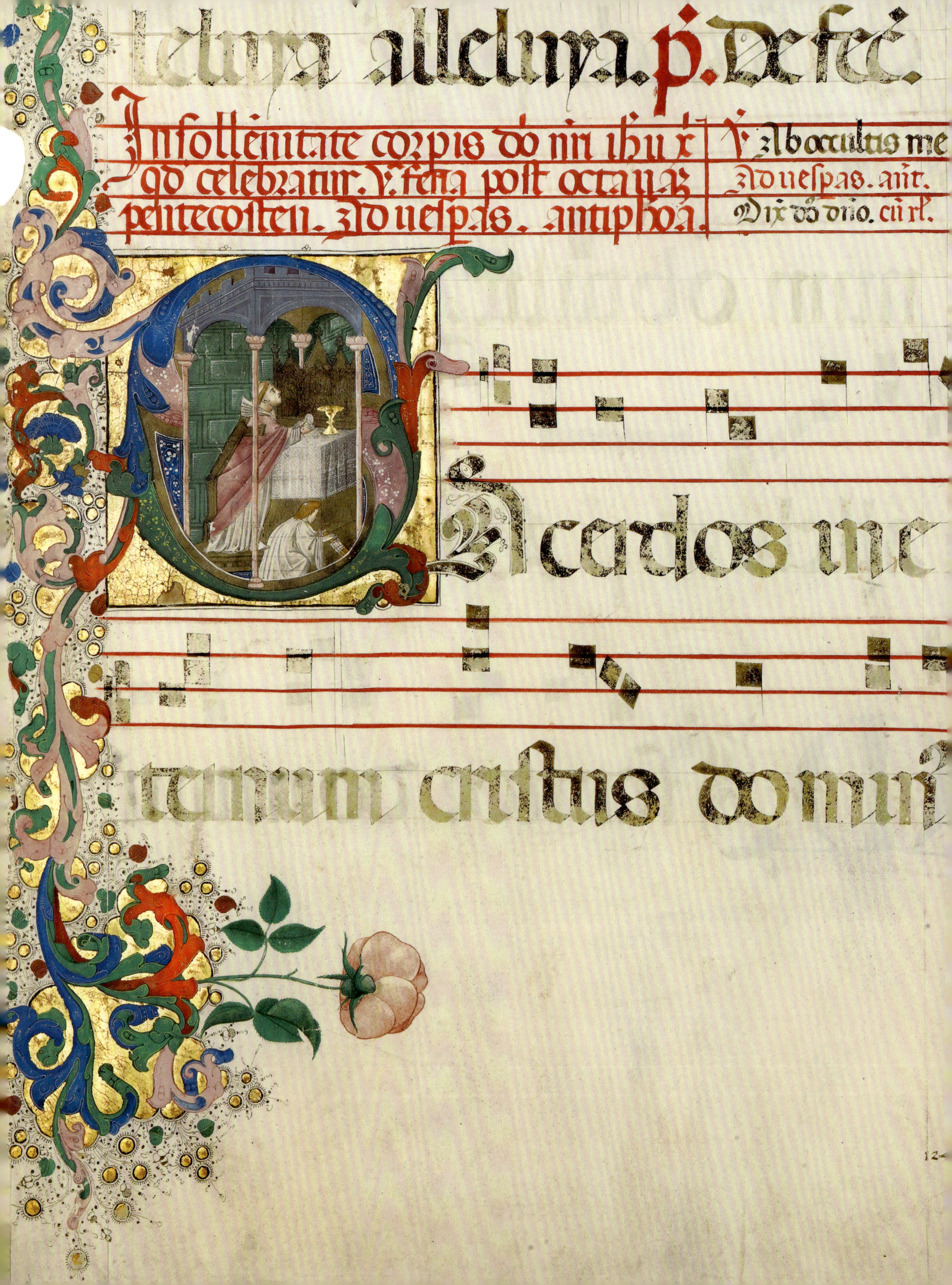
leluya alleluya. P. Defec.
In sollemnitate corporis domini nostri ihesu christi quod celebratur V. feria post octavam penthecosten. Ad vespas. antiphona.
V. Ab occultis me
Ad vespas. ant.
Dix dns dno. cu rl.
Sacerdos ine
ternum cristus domin

# Choirs of Angels

## PAINTING IN ITALIAN CHOIR BOOKS, 1300–1500

BARBARA DRAKE BOEHM

The Metropolitan Museum of Art, New York
Yale University Press, New Haven and London

Reprint of *The Metropolitan Museum of Art Bulletin* (Winter 2009).


This publication is made possible through the generosity of the Lila Acheson Wallace Fund for The Metropolitan Museum of Art, established by the cofounder of *Reader's Digest*.

This publication is issued in conjunction with the exhibition "Choirs of Angels: Painting in Italian Choir Books, 1300–1500," held at The Metropolitan Museum of Art, New York, from November 25, 2008, to April 12, 2009.

The exhibition is made possible by the Michel David-Weill Fund.

Publisher and Editor in Chief: John P. O'Neill
Editor of the *Bulletin*: Sue Potter
Production: Christopher Zichello
Design: Bruce Campbell

Cover: Attributed to Cosmè Tura (1430?–1495). *Initial A with the Assumption of the Virgin*. Ferrara, 1450–60 (see fig. 26). Frontispiece: Master of the Riccardiana Lactantius. Leaf from a Benedictine antiphonary with *The Celebration of a Mass in an Initial S* (detail). Florence, second half of 15th century (see fig. 16)

Cataloging-in-Publication data is available from the Library of Congress.
ISBN: 978-1-58839-305-0 (The Metropolitan Museum of Art)
ISBN: 978-0-300-14142-9 (Yale University Press)



Printed and bound in the United States of America.

# Director's Note

The illuminated choir book is one of the great legacies of Western culture, a unique marriage of two great achievements of the Middle Ages—the illumination of books and the codified system of musical notation. Intended for monasteries and cathedrals half a millennium ago, these exquisite manuscripts are still captivating today. Most were removed from massive bound volumes in the Napoleonic era, and their brilliant colors and shining gold surfaces have attracted connoisseurs ever since. For the art historian, these illuminations bear witness to exceptional aesthetic accomplishment. For the musicologist, choir books provide a rich source in the history of notation and the development of chant, the transcendent tonalities of which have great contemporary appeal. For the historian, choir books serve as primary sources in the study of the lives of religious communities and the philosophy and faith that infused medieval Europe. And most important, for visitors to the Museum, our choral manuscripts exemplify the extraordinary creativity of artists in Italy on the eve of the Renaissance.

The illuminated pages presented here constitute a collection formed over more than a century, sometimes by design and often by serendipity. By the time the Metropolitan was founded in 1870, the collecting of single leaves and initials from choral manuscripts was already a venerable tradition. In England the pattern first established by such great English antiquarians as Francis Douce, William Beckford, John Ruskin, and William Young Ottley and the Scotsman James Dennistoun (the latter two once owners of works in the Metropolitan's collection) was flourishing before the mid-nineteenth century. Collectors of early Renaissance panel paintings remarked the importance of manuscript illumination in the history of painting, William Ottley noting that certain artists "occasionally condescended to paint in miniature."

The first illumination acquired by the Metropolitan was as a gift in 1888 from Coudert Brothers, a Manhattan law firm eager to dispose of works of art given to them by an appreciative Florentine client. Only recently has that letter V illustrated with an image of Joseph being sold by his brothers (fig. 49) been recognized as the work of Giovanni Pietro da Cemmo, a painter and illuminator who created works for Augustinian foundations in Brescia, Crema, and Cremona. In 1890 another surprise donation arrived from the daughter of Mrs. A. M. Minturn, who humbly wrote, "If any of these articles should not be deemed worthy [of] the acceptance of the Museum, kindly notify me." Among the "articles" in Mrs. Minturn's bequest were a leaf from a Venetian choir book from about 1400 (fig. 32) and an image of Saint Lawrence by Don Simone (fig. 35), one of the most celebrated illuminators in Tuscany in the late fourteenth century. The year 1896 brought sixteen leaves as the gift of Louis L. Lorillard, including the glorious *Assumption of the Virgin* by Niccolò di ser Sozzo (fig. 40) and leaves from a sumptuous Florentine antiphonary from the last half of the fifteenth century, five of which are illustrated here (figs. 16, 19, 38, 39, 53).

In the early twentieth century Bryson Burroughs, curator of paintings at the Museum (and painter of the frescoes commissioned for the vestibule of the Century Association in New York for its seventy-fifth anniversary celebration), recommended the purchase of some of our most important miniatures: the imposing Easter scenes by the Bolognese illuminator Nerius (fig. 42), the delicate *Virgin and Child* by the Master of the Franciscan Breviary (fig. 74), four masterful initials linked to the Ferrarese painter Cosmè Tura (figs. 26–29), and the *Birth of the Virgin* now recognized as the work of Don Silvestro dei Gherarducci (fig. 47). Created for one of the great choir books of Santa Maria degli Angeli in Florence in about 1375, the Don Silvestro illumination was purchased in 1921 for £50, a tenth the price of a panel painting bought at the same time from the same dealer.

After Burroughs's retirement, and subsequent to the opening of the Pierpont Morgan Library in 1924, the Metropolitan deliberately steered away from the purchase of books and single leaves. The acquisition of choral illuminations depended almost entirely on unanticipated gifts from New York area collectors whose remarkable generosity has both enriched and shaped the Museum's collection: Bradish Johnson Carroll, whose gifts are identified here for the first time as works from Imola Cathedral; Gwynne M. Andrews; and Millie Bruhl Frederick, an American portrait painter who upon her death at age eighty-four bequeathed an exquisite cutting with *The Holy Women at the Tomb* now attributed to Girolamo dai Libri (fig. 44). A small but brilliant group of illuminations in the collection came from Bashford Dean, honorary curator of arms and armor at the Metropolitan from 1906 to 1927, who assembled them for his personal collection specifically because they depict medieval armor. Especially appealing among them is the Bolognese *Initial A with the Battle of the Maccabees* (fig. 52). The most avid of the collectors affiliated with the Metropolitan was Robert Lehman, some of whose illuminations are housed in the collection at the Museum that bears his name and some in the Department of Medieval Art and The Cloisters. An anonymous loan to the department offers an important example of illumination from the circle of Neri da Rimini. Recent gifts sponsored by the department's Visiting Committee, notably Elaine Rosenberg, Ronald R. Atkins, James Marrow, and Austin B. Chinn, have substantially augmented the breadth and quality of the Metropolitan's assemblage of choir books.

This issue of the *Bulletin* was written by Barbara Drake Boehm, Curator in the Department of Medieval Art and The Cloisters. In conjunction with this publication, forty of the most salient examples of Italian choir book illumination in the Metropolitan's collection will be exhibited in the Medieval Sculpture Hall. The exhibition has been made possible through the generous support of the Michel David-Weill Fund.

Philippe de Montebello
*Director*

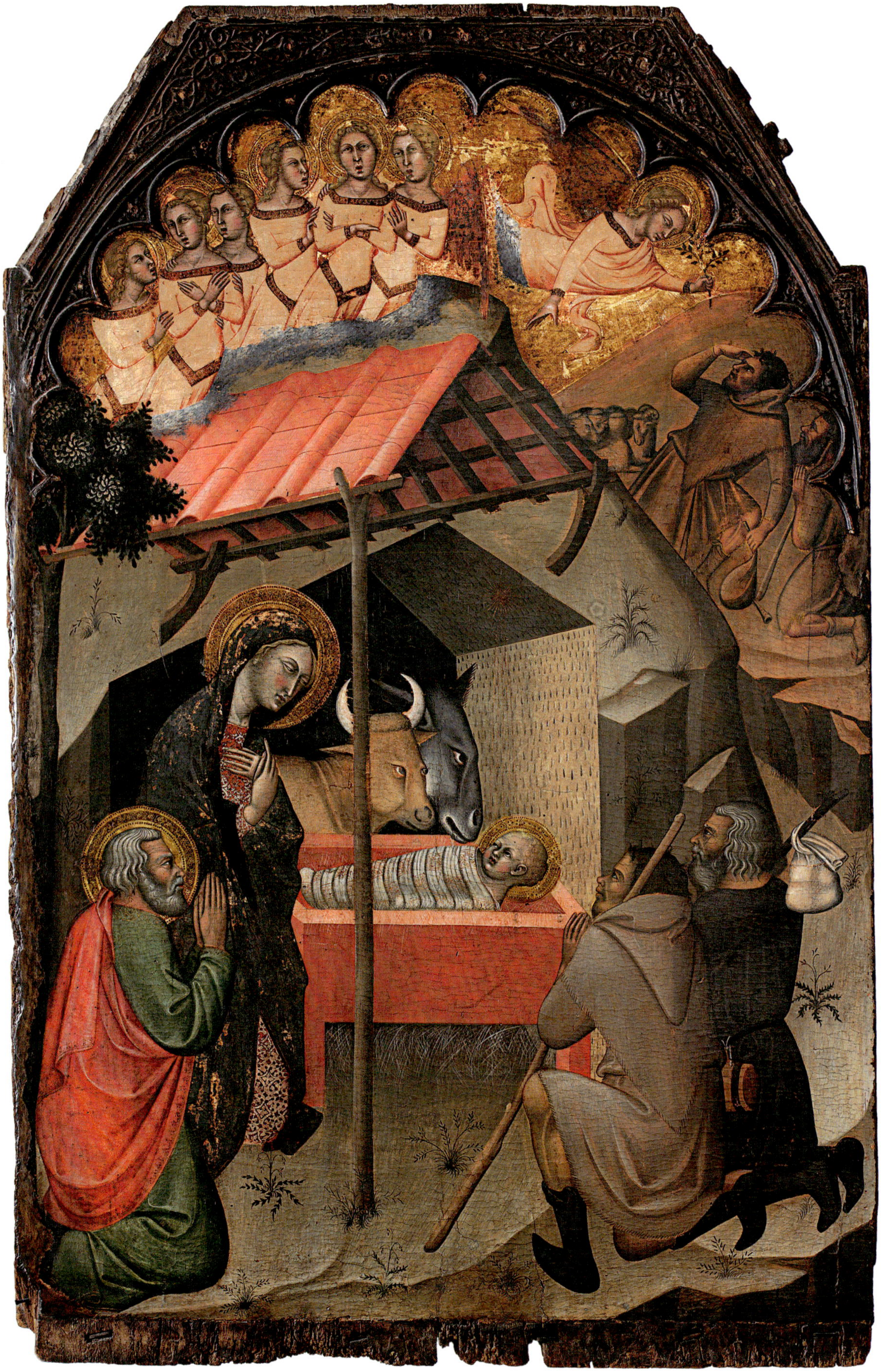

# Choirs of Angels

## PAINTING IN ITALIAN CHOIR BOOKS, 1300–1500

*We mingle our praises with those of God's angels, which we cannot hear.*
—Cassiodorus

As Christmas approaches every year, performances of Handel's *Messiah* take place across the country and around the world. Program notes frequently recount that during twenty-four intense days in the summer of 1741 the composer was seized by a kind of religious fervor, locking himself in his study, breaking for neither food nor drink, and hearing angelic voices: "I did think I did see all Heaven before me, and the great God himself."[1] Handel's account conforms to an enduring Christian tradition that associates music with the presence of God. It can be found in the gospel account of the birth of Jesus (Luke 2:13), and it echoes through Handel's own oratorio. It is repeatedly invoked in Christian art, perhaps nowhere more lyrically than in Italian painting on the eve of the Renaissance. In Bartolo di Fredi's *Adoration of the Shepherds* (fig. 1), for example, the heavenly nature of the baby born in a humble manger is emphatically confirmed by the white-robed angels singing in the golden sky overhead.

In a broader sense, the perceived links between music and the divine are arguably universal. The concept is inherent in the ancient Greek legend of Orpheus, whose songs were so beautiful that they could charm wild beasts and persuade Hades to release his wife from the underworld. Even in a modern, secular context, there is clearly something we do not fully understand about the creative spark and the power of music. In *Musicophilia: Tales of Music and the Brain* the neuroscientist Oliver Sacks recounts the story of a physician with almost no musical training who after being struck by lightning began to transcribe original musical compositions he heard inside his head.[2] In the Middle Ages such a marvelous account would have confirmed the absolute conviction that music connects us to the divine. That belief is explicit in an art form that emerged across medieval and Renaissance Europe: the illuminated choir book.

At a distance of more than half a millennium, it is difficult to convey the sheer volume of production that was involved in meeting the demand for richly painted choir books that developed from the late thirteenth century to the dawn of the sixteenth. By way of example, at the cathedral of Florence alone, thirty-three volumes were commissioned over a period of sixteen years, beginning in 1508.[3] The volumes required the participation of more than sixty artists and craftsmen charged with tasks as varied as providing the parchment (one goatskin was required per page),[4] writing the text, transcribing the music, decorating the borders, painting the initials, gilding the initials, covering the bindings with silk or wool, and applying metal clasps.[5] The production of the multivolume set of choir books for Santa Maria degli Angeli in Florence (see figs. 47, 59, 60), admired by the historian Giorgio Vasari as works of great refinement, continued over a period of 135 years and was in fact never completed.[6] Thirteen volumes listed in fifteenth-century inventories of the church of San Domenico in Perugia survive, each with about two hundred pages and about two feet tall.[7] Visitors to the Piccolomini Library (fig. 2) of Siena Cathedral can see in the magnificent volumes now assembled there the colossal nature of these commissions: twenty-nine volumes, each about three feet high and more than three feet across when opened. They were first commissioned in 1457; by 1468, eighteen had been completed.[8]

Whether still in churches or dispersed in museums and private collections, illustrated choir books represent a remarkable art form, a unique marriage of the visual and musical arts. Individual pages are often opulent in their use of brilliant color and

1. Bartolo di Fredi (active 1353, died 1410). *The Adoration of the Shepherds*. Siena, ca. 1374. Tempera on poplar, gilding; painted surface 63 ¼ x 45 ⅛ in. (160.7 x 114.6 cm). The Metropolitan Museum of Art, The Cloisters Collection, 1925 (25.120.288)

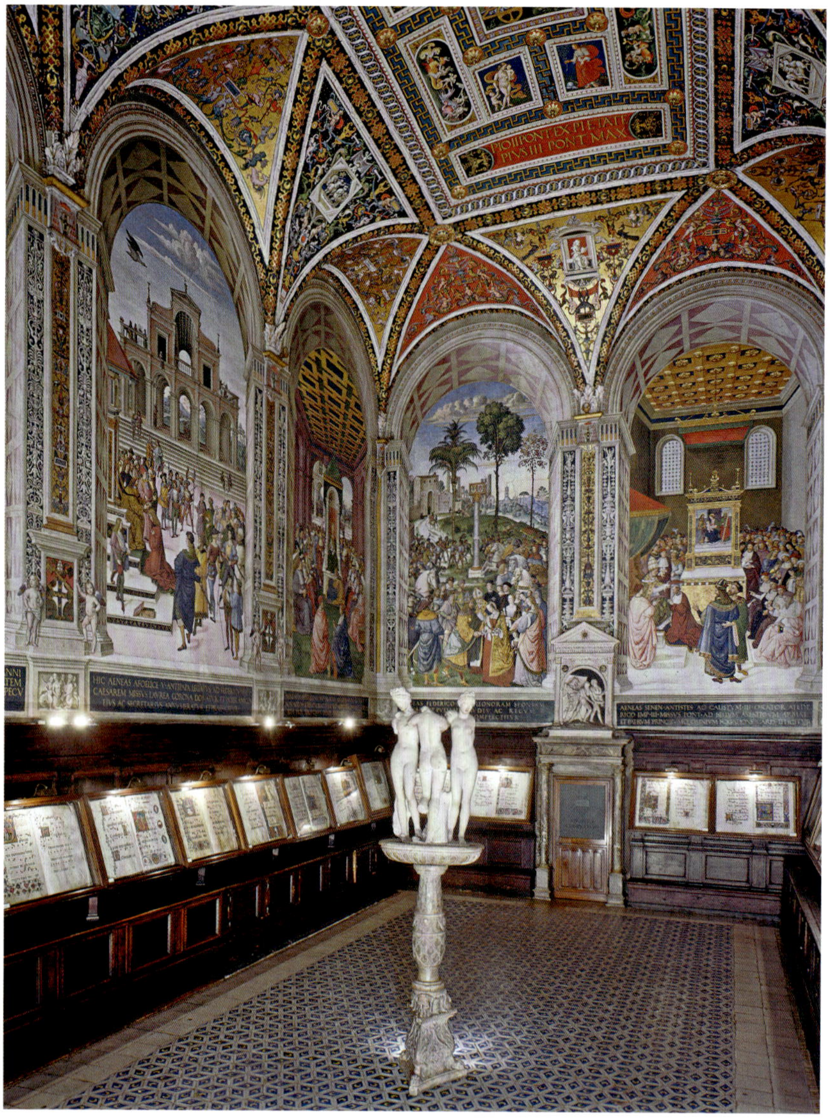

2. Choir books displayed on lecterns in the Piccolomini Library, Siena Cathedral

gold. Their imagery is at times conservative, at times innovative; their painting is sometimes masterful and sometimes merely workmanlike. The Metropolitan's relatively small collection, consisting mostly of single leaves and cuttings from choir books, nonetheless hints at the importance and ubiquity of choral music in Italy in the fourteenth and fifteenth centuries. An almost insatiable, pervasive taste for illuminated musical manuscripts obtained across a wide swath of the Italian peninsula, especially in wealthy cities and duchies, from Florence, Siena, and Lucca in Tuscany to Perugia in Umbria to Bologna, Ferrara, Venice, and Verona in the northeast to Milan and Cremona in the north (see maps, pages 60–61).

The Metropolitan's collection, like those in other museums around the world, developed from connoisseurs' interest in these precious illuminations as beautiful small paintings. For more than two centuries collectors have recognized them as the work of important artists, painting on parchment rather than panel. The English collector William Young Ottley, who lived in Italy for a decade beginning in 1791, noted that Italian "illuminists, or Miniature Painters," were often "of a superior order" and that, though small in scale, "these specimens are, in many cases, found in a more perfect state of preservation than the frescoes and other large works of painting remaining to us of the same periods."[9] A nineteenth-century English enthusiast, the Reverend Thomas Frognall Dibdin, proclaimed that in choir books "Giotto, Cimabue, and a hundred other graphic constellations of various degrees of magnitude and luster, diffused their grateful light. . . . There is no doubt that the Popes and Cardinals of the time procured the most distinguished artists to decorate their Missals or Books of Church Service."[10]

## The Napoleonic Suppression

*These beautiful books . . . fell into the hands of some boors*

At the time these Englishmen were voicing their enthusiasm for Italian choral manuscripts they were quite easy to acquire. Between 1796 and 1799, coincident with the years William Ottley lived in Italy, French armies under Napoleon occupied the Italian peninsula. A puppet government was established in Lombardy, and in 1798 the Milanese republic abolished the monasteries and sold most of their land. That same year Pope Pius VI was sent into exile, dying in France the following year. The year 1799 saw the partial suppression of monastic establishments in Piedmont, and the abolition of nearly all of them in Lombardy, Tuscany, and the former Papal States. Virtually overnight there was no one using or safeguarding the long-treasured choir books. Within a decade some had entered nearby cathedral libraries, some (as in France after the Revolution) had become the property of local civic libraries, and some had migrated to dealers and collectors. The monks of Santa Maria degli Angeli in Florence seem themselves to have sold parts of one choir book to William Ottley, including the Metropolitan's *Birth of the Virgin* (see fig. 47) and nineteen other glorious miniatures by Don Silvestro dei Gherarducci, before the remains of the bound volume entered the Laurentian Library in

Florence in 1809.[11] Similarly, the Scotsman James Dennistoun purchased illuminations by Niccolò di Giacomo, including the Metropolitan's *Martyrdom of Saint Stephen* (fig. 3), directly from the Carthusian community outside Lucca during a visit there.[12] Dennistoun perceived his acquisitions as part of an ongoing salvaging effort: "On the invasion of Italy by the revolutionary armies of France, these beautiful books were plundered, and fell into the hands of some boors, who proceeded to cut up the broad parchment leaves, wherewith to cover their flasks of olive oil. Fortunately, someone rather less barbarous rescued these initials by crudely cutting them out, without the slightest regard to the elegant borders, which are crudely mangled. The collection thus saved was bought by me at Lucca in 1838."[13]

Choral manuscripts were unwieldy, with their heavy protective bindings made of wooden boards wrapped with leather and studded with metal fastenings. The Reverend Dibdin noted that "at a late sale . . . by Messrs. Leigh and Sotheby (May 1, 1816) there were several lots of entire volumes of these *Chants* and *Services*, of a bulk and breadth that forbade ordinary shoulders to bear them away."[14] The British government's import duty on manuscripts based on their weight therefore provided ample incentive to separate individual leaves or miniatures from their heavy and often worn, unattractive bindings.[15]

Some medieval bound choir books were undoubtedly already in poor condition by the nineteenth century. When the community of San Giacomo Maggiore in Bologna was suppressed in 1866, long after many other monasteries had been closed, the friars secreted three choir books beneath the altar of Saint Bartholomew, hoping to save them. The manuscripts were discovered in 1885, when the altar was moved as part of an effort to clean the church, but by then they had suffered from the humidity and were covered with mold and dust (fig. 4).[16] Some of the miniatures from the San Giacomo choir books were sold to dealers, and some were acquired by the Museo Civico Medievale in Bologna. The books have recently undergone restoration, and a number of the individual cuttings have now been restored to their original bound volumes.[17] To cite a more recent example, the sixteenth-century choir books belonging to the cathedral of Florence were seriously damaged during the catastrophic flooding of the River Arno in 1966.

Because choir books were such an integral part of the church service, they were also subject to damage from use. For example, the account books of the basilica of Saint Francis at Assisi for 1358 include payments not only for the purchase of new books but also for the repair of an antiphonary.[18] In fact, over the centuries choir books were removed from church collections for many reasons. A choir book was useful only as long as its contents conformed to the needs of a service. Some choir books became obsolete, for instance, after the Council of Trent of 1545–63, when a number of feasts were removed from the calendar of the Roman Catholic Church and the music of hymns was altered or chants particular to a diocese were eliminated.[19] Once the service changed, the original text was valuable only insofar as its materials could be recycled. Earlier parchment was thus sometimes reused as binding material, as when a twelfth-century antiphonary leaf was bound into a later book in the cathedral of Florence.[20]

Other equally dire fates befell precious medieval manuscripts. On December 29, 1698, long before antiquarian collectors took an interest in choir book illuminations, a choir book painted about

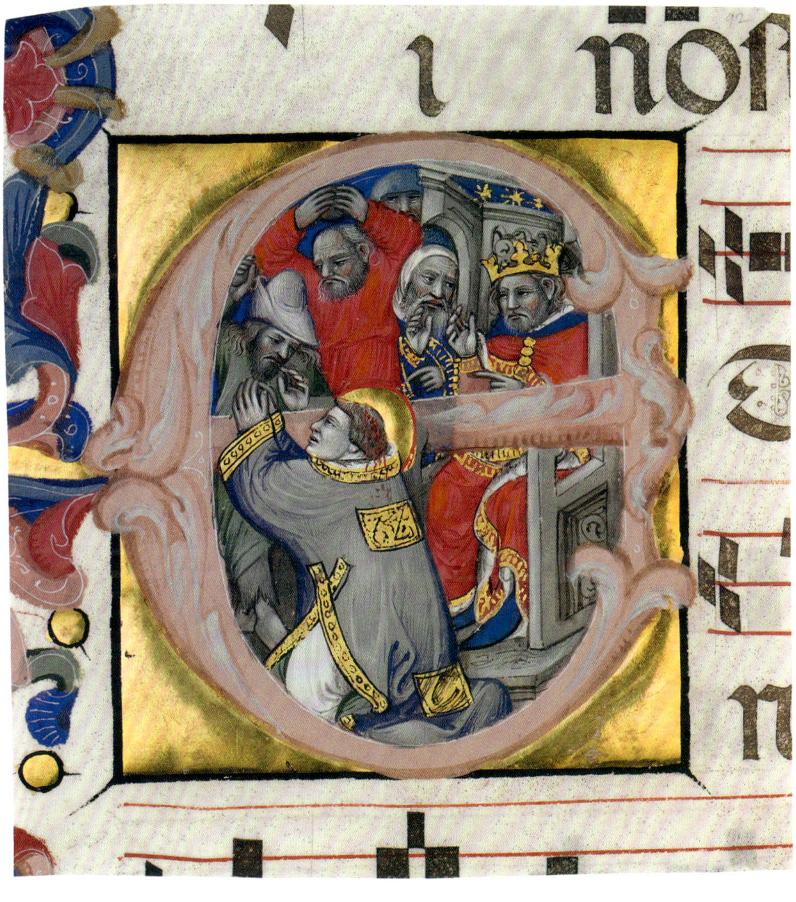

3. Niccolò di Giacomo da Bologna (active 1349–1403). *Initial E with the Martyrdom of Saint Stephen*. Bologna, ca. 1394–1402. From a gradual created for the Certosa dello Spirito Santo at Farneta, near Lucca. Tempera, gold, and ink on parchment; 7 ½ x 6 7/8 in. (19 x 17.6 cm). The Metropolitan Museum of Art, Purchase, Gift of George Blumenthal, by exchange, Elaine Rosenberg and Austin B. Chinn Gifts, and Bequest of Fannie F. Einstein, in memory of Emanuel Einstein, by exchange, 2007 (2007.236)

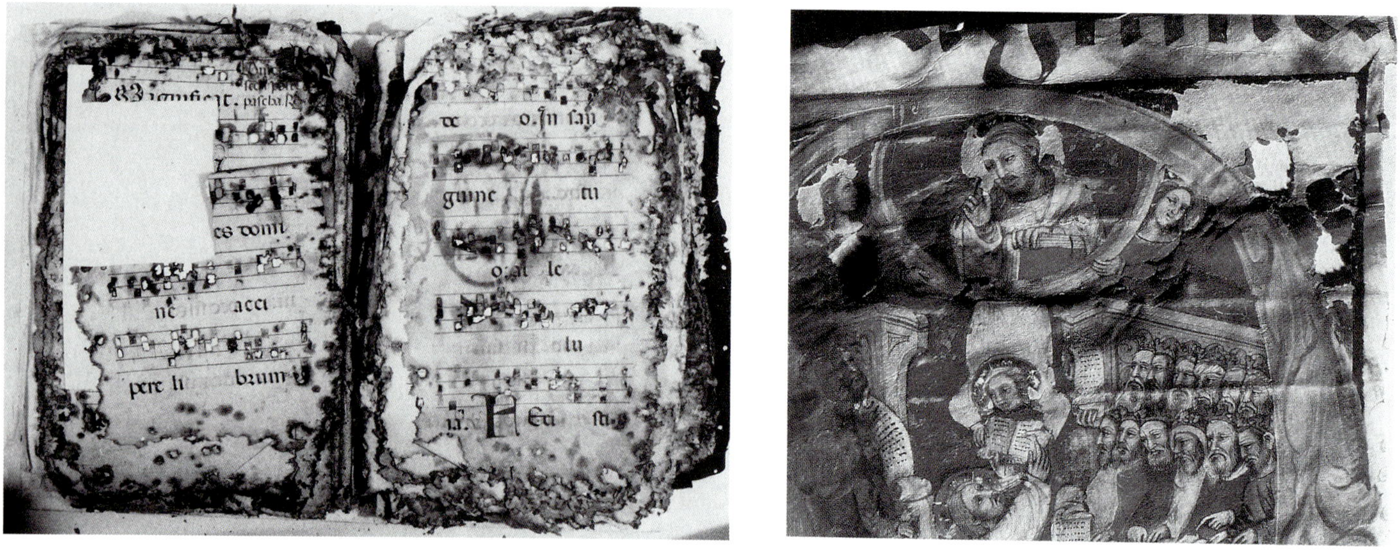

4. *Left:* Antiphonary created for the Augustinian monastery of San Giacomo Maggiore, Bologna, before restoration. *Right:* Niccolò di Giacomo da Bologna, *Initial D with the Revelation of the Apocalypse*, cut from the left page of the antiphonary shown here, before restoration. Bologna, 14th century. Tempera, gold, and ink on parchment; each folio 23 ¼ x 15 ⅜ in. (59 x 39 cm). Museo Civico Medievale, Bologna (ms. 4109, fols. 179v–180r)

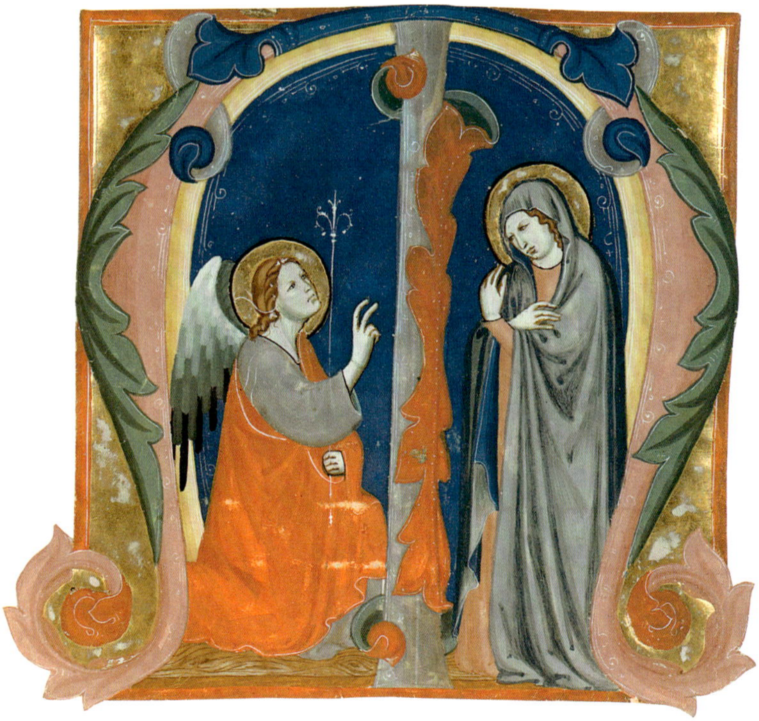

5. Maestro Daddesco(?) (active first half of 14th century). *Initial M with the Annunciation.* Florence, ca. 1310–15. From an antiphonary. Tempera, gold, and ink on parchment; 5 ⅜ x 5 ¼ in. (13.6 x 13.4 cm). The Metropolitan Museum of Art, Robert Lehman Collection, 1975 (1975.1.2478)

1330 by the Maestro Daddesco, the artist also probably responsible for the cutting with the Annunciation in the Metropolitan (fig. 5), was stolen from the lectern in the choir of Florence Cathedral. An impoverished citizen named Simone de Francesco Merlini seized the manuscript in order to sell its mounts to a scrap-metal dealer. As he fled, he ripped the illuminated leaves from their binding, eventually abandoning some on the streets and jettisoning others into the River Arno from the Santa Trinità Bridge.[21]

### Music in the Church
*Sing, choirs of angels*

The foundation for the integral role of singing in Christian worship lies in Jewish tradition. The singing of psalms was an essential part of worship in Jerusalem in both the First Temple (built by Solomon in the tenth century B.C.E. and destroyed by the Babylonians in 586 B.C.E) and the Second (dedicated in 515 B.C.E. and destroyed by the Romans in 70 C.E.).[22] The Second Temple choir included at least twelve adult members of the Levite tribe, joined by younger voices and accompanied by trumpets and cymbals.[23] Traditional Jewish sources maintain that the playing of music ceased after the destruction of the Second Temple. The Talmud, the central text of Jewish law and tradition compiled in the early sixth century, cites Lamentations 5:14 as the authority for this: "The old men are gone from the gate, the young men from their music." Music praising God was not prohibited, however. Thus although a twelfth-century legal code like Maimonides' *Mishneh Torah* forbade instrumental music, it also stated that it is customary to sing praises to God.[24]

Apparently perpetuating the tradition of Jewish ceremonial meals rather than formal worship services, the singing of hymns by early Christians seems to have been associated with the sharing of meals within the fledgling community.[25] The gospels attest to the use of music among the followers of Jesus. Saint Matthew (26:30) and Saint Mark

(14:26) indicate that Jesus and his disciples sang a hymn at the conclusion of the Last Supper, at which, in keeping with their Jewish tradition, they shared the Passover meal. The Roman historian Pliny the Younger wrote to the emperor Trajan (r. 98–117) that Christians "were wont to assemble on a set day before dawn and to sing a hymn among themselves . . . to the Christ, as to a god . . . , after which it was their custom to separate and to come together again to take food."[26] The early Christian writer Tertullian (ca. 160–225) claimed that Christian husbands and wives "challenge each other to see who better sings to the Lord."[27] References to singing as part of a formal service of worship are later. A late fourth-century pilgrim to Jerusalem named Egeria described in her diary the prayer services in Jerusalem at which "hymns are sung and psalms are responded to."[28]

Medieval Christians repeatedly acknowledged their music's debt to the heritage of the biblical king David, whose image is pervasive in illuminated music manuscripts. In a northern Italian example (fig. 6), David, with a graying beard and ruddy complexion and wearing a slightly exotic turban, appears alongside the letter I of the beginning of Psalm 85. He holds a pen, signaling his importance as the author of the Psalms rather than as a king. The face of God and his voice, rendered as undulating waves suggesting breath, appear in the sky overhead, and at the top of the I is a curious small fish—an allusion to the Christian faith? The text conveys David's humility as he petitions God: "Incline thy ear, O Lord, and hear me for I am needy and poor." In counterpoint to the text, in the illumination it is David, not God, who inclines his head. Another image of David in prayer appears in a letter M illuminated by Girolamo dai Libri for the Olivetan monastery of Santa Maria in Organo in Verona (fig. 7).

David was regarded as the father of medieval music. Biblical texts remark his playing for his flock as a young shepherd, soothing King Saul with his music, and playing before the Ark of the Covenant.[29] The fifteenth-century marble pavement in the nave of Siena Cathedral (fig. 8) includes a prominent image proclaiming David's role as a musician. The artist, probably Domenico di Niccolò, bound biblical instrumental practice to Christian liturgy that focused on vocal music: with an open book of music on a lectern at his side and surrounded by four young musicians playing instruments and singing, David

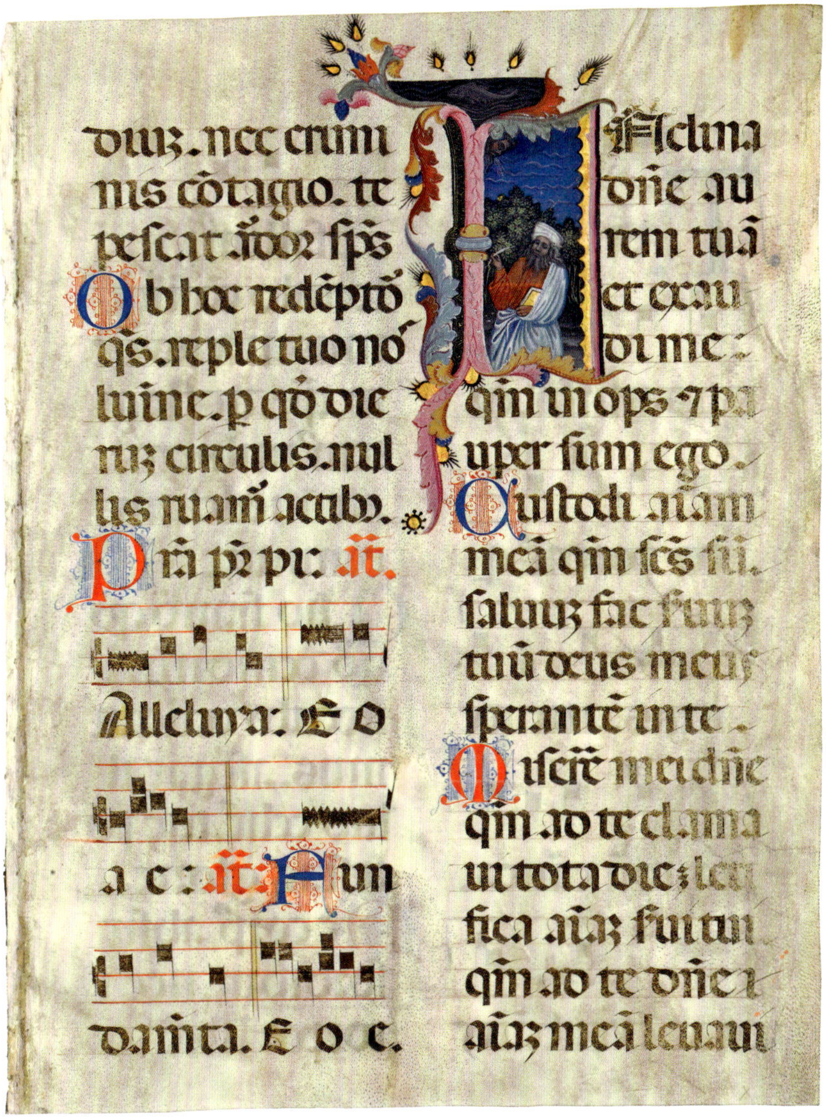

6. Leaf from a psalter with *King David in an Initial I*. Northern Italy, early 15th century. Tempera, gold, and ink on parchment; 18 1/8 x 13 7/8 in. (46 x 35.1 cm). The Metropolitan Museum of Art, Gift of Miss Alice M. Dike, in memory of her father, Henry A. Dike, 1928 (28.225.65)

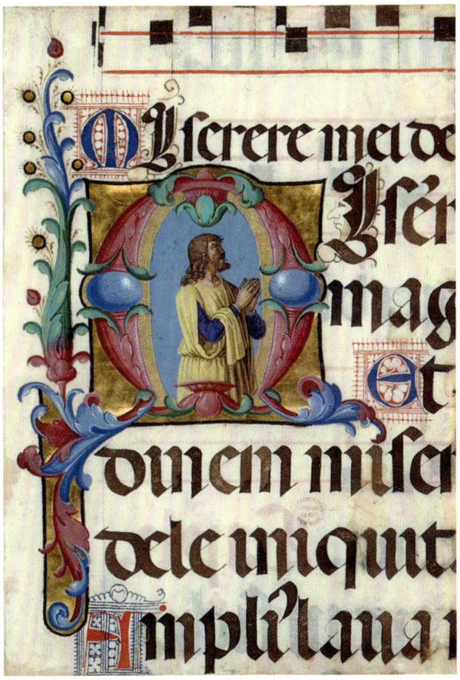

7. Girolamo dai Libri (1474/75–1555?). *Initial M with David in Prayer*. Verona, 1501–2. From a psalter created for the Olivetan monastery of Santa Maria in Organo, Verona. Tempera, gold, and ink on parchment; 9 x 6 1/4 in. (22.7 x 15.9 cm). The Metropolitan Museum of Art, Rogers Fund, 1912 (12.56.3)

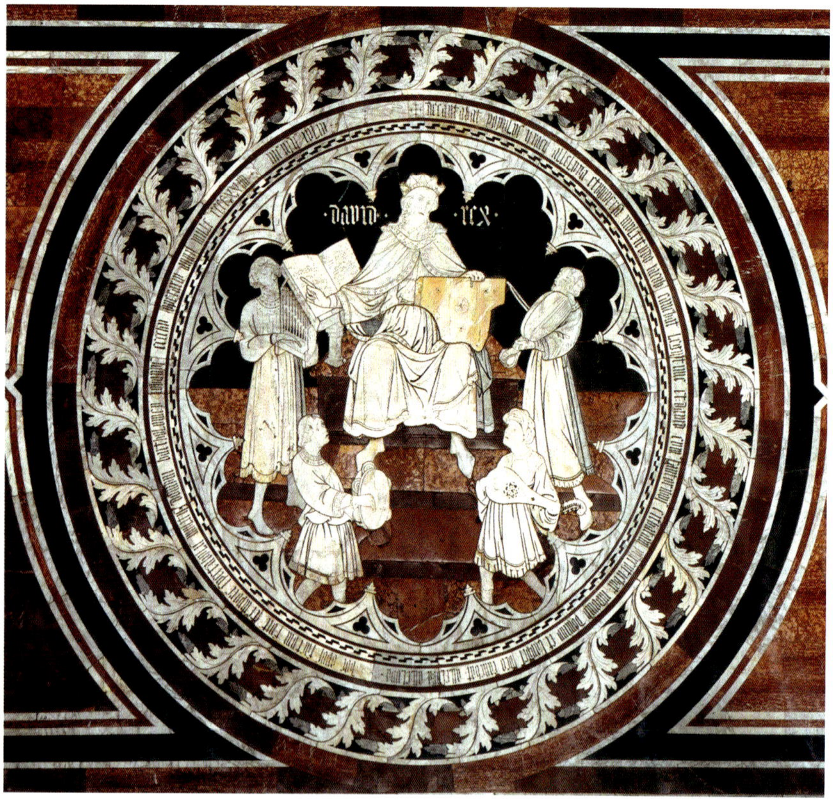

8. Attributed to Domenico di Niccolò (1363–before 1453). *David the Psalmist and Musicians.* Tondo in the marble pavement of Siena Cathedral

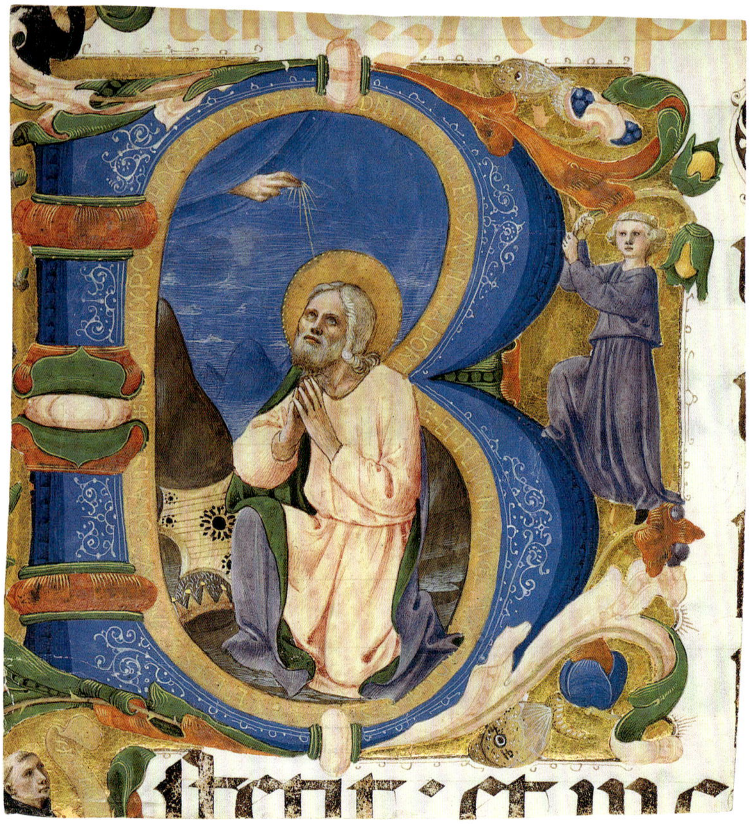

9. Zanobi Strozzi (1412–1468). *Initial B with King David in Prayer.* Florence, ca. 1450. From a Benedictine psalter. Tempera, gold, and ink on parchment; 5⅝ x 5⅜ in. (14.2 x 13.5 cm). The Metropolitan Museum of Art, Robert Lehman Collection, 1975 (1975.1.2470)

balances his psaltery (a medieval stringed instrument) on his knee as he assumes the role of cantor, or choir director.

The Florentine illuminator Zanobi Strozzi represented David at the moment God inspired him (fig. 9). David has set his crown on the ground, next to his psaltery. As God's hand emerges from a cloud, the rays of gold descending from his fingertip seem to create David's halo, his chief attribute. The scene elucidates the opening of Psalm 1: "Blessed is the man who hath not walked in the counsel of the ungodly, nor stood in the way of sinners, nor sat in the chair of pestilence." The Benedictine monk partially visible below the initial is emblematic of the community for which the book was made. He raises his gaze reverently to David, the legendary wellspring of monastic musical practice.

## The Practice of Music

***Seven times a day I praise thee for thy righteous ordinances***

The singing of psalms became part of the daily regimen of communities of early Christian monks. At the dawn of the fourth century Saint Athanasius of Alexandria wrote that "there were monasteries in the mountains, like tabernacles, filled with saintly choirs reciting psalms, devoutly reading, fasting, praying, rejoicing in the hope of things to come, and laboring to give alms, while maintaining love and harmony among themselves."[30] An anonymous fourth-century Greek theologian known as Pseudo-Chrysostom reported that in keeping with the tradition of David, both nuns and monks established communion with the angels through their singing: "In the monasteries there is a holy chorus of angelic hosts, and David is first, middle and last. In the convents there are bands of virgins who imitate Mary, and David is first, middle and last. In the deserts men crucified to this world converse with God, and David is first, middle and last."[31] Basil the Great, the fourth-century bishop of Caesarea and father of communal monasticism in the Eastern Church, praised the beneficial effects of the Book of Psalms as a builder of community: "A psalm is tranquility of soul and the arbitrarion of peace; . . . it mollifies the soul's wrath and chastens its recalcitrance. A psalm creates friendships, unites the separated and reconciles those at enmity. . . . Psalmody provides the greatest of all goods, charity, by devising in its common song a certain bond of unity, and by joining together the people into the concord of a single chorus."[32]

The *Liber Pontificalis,* which records the accomplishments of the popes, credits Pope Celestine I (r. 422–32) with a key role in establishing the importance of the psalms in the celebration of the Eucharist (Holy Communion).[33] Saint Benedict (ca. 480–543), whose *Rule* codified the daily regimen of prayer and work (*Ora et Labor*) for monasteries across Western Europe, specified that the "full number of 150 Psalms be chanted every week and begun again every Sunday at the Night Office." He complained about those who did not live up to expectations: "For those monks show themselves too lazy in the service to which they are vowed, who chant less than the Psalter with the customary canticles in the course of a week, whereas we read that our holy Fathers strenuously fulfilled that task in a single day. May we, lukewarm that we are, perform it at least in a whole week."[34] Illuminations in choir books repeatedly show monks fulfilling the duty articulated by Saint Benedict centuries before. In one of Girolamo dai Libri's illuminations for a psalter for the Olivetan monastery of Santa Maria in Organo (fig. 10), three monks sing prayerfully. Rays of gold descend to them from heaven, making explicit the path their music provides to God. In the preface to his *Exposito psalmorum* (Commentary on the Psalms), the great Roman statesman Cassiodorus (ca. 485–ca. 585), himself a lover of manuscripts and a champion of the written word, extolled "the psalms which make our vigils pleasant, when a human voice, breaking the silence of the night, bursts forth from the choir of those who sing the psalms."[35]

Children preparing for monastic life memorized the psalter and, prior to the development of musical notation, the accompanying chants as well. In fact, as the scholar Isidore of Seville remarked in the seventh century, the melodies could not be written down.[36] By 747 a council at Clovesho, England, had decreed that all churches should follow the liturgical chant as set out in a songbook sent from Rome,[37] but whether the book contained both text and notation is not clear. Until the eleventh century the repertory of hymn texts was limited, and books with musical notation appear to have been rare exceptions.[38]

The standardization of text and music into what is known as Gregorian chant developed as a consequence of liturgical reforms implemented by Charlemagne. On March 23, 789, reiterating a directive of his father, Pépin the Short, the king instructed the clergy to replace the regional tradition of Gaul with Roman chant. The name of Gregory, who was identified with Pope Gregory I (r. 590–604) and celebrated as an author of hymns, served as a kind of imprimatur, lending authority to the earliest Frankish chant books.[39] Charlemagne further ordained that schools be established to teach boys to read. Chants were included in the curriculum as part of the literacy requirement, perhaps along with an early form of musical notation now lost to us.[40] Bringing the musical repertory into conformity was apparently grueling work that continued into the reign of Charlemagne's son Louis the Pious. According to Amalarius, bishop of

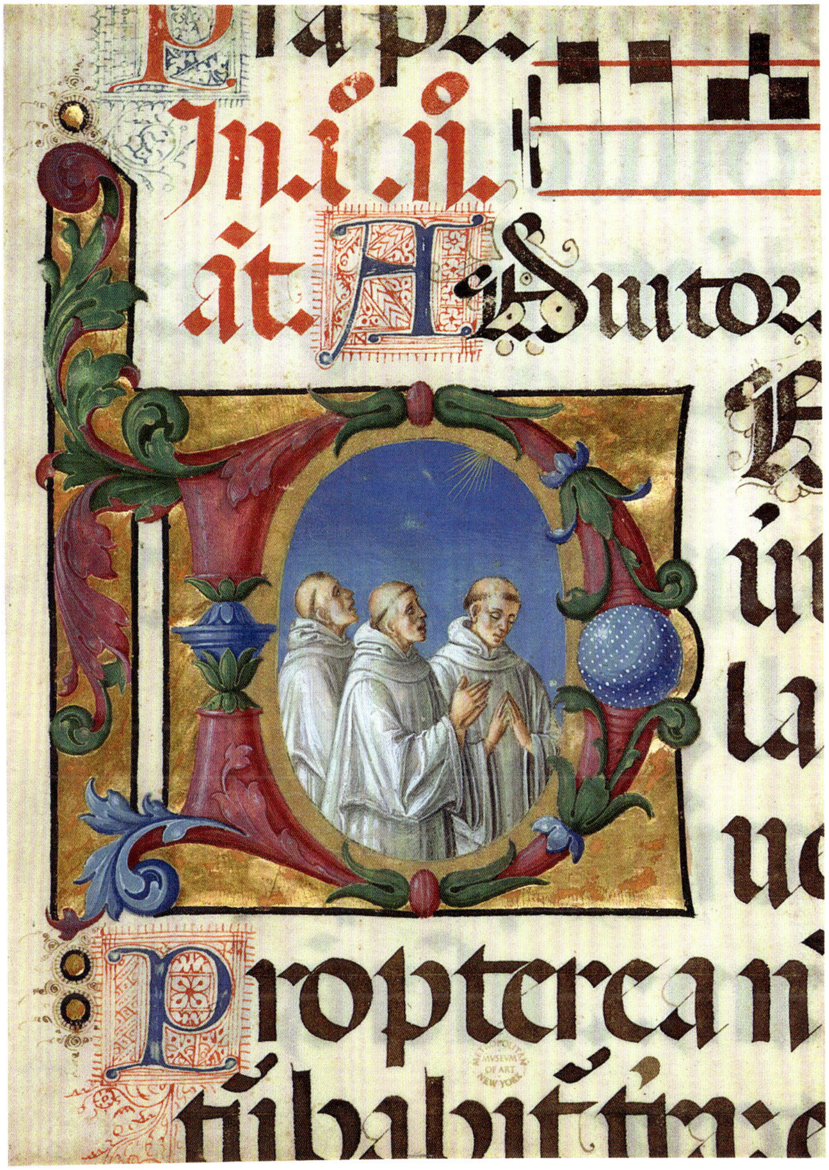

10. Girolamo dai Libri. *Initial D with Singing Monks.* Verona, 1501–2. From a psalter created for the Olivetan monastery of Santa Maria in Organo, Verona. Tempera, gold, and ink on parchment; 9 x 7 in. (23 x 17.8 cm). The Metropolitan Museum of Art, Rogers Fund, 1912 (12.56.4)

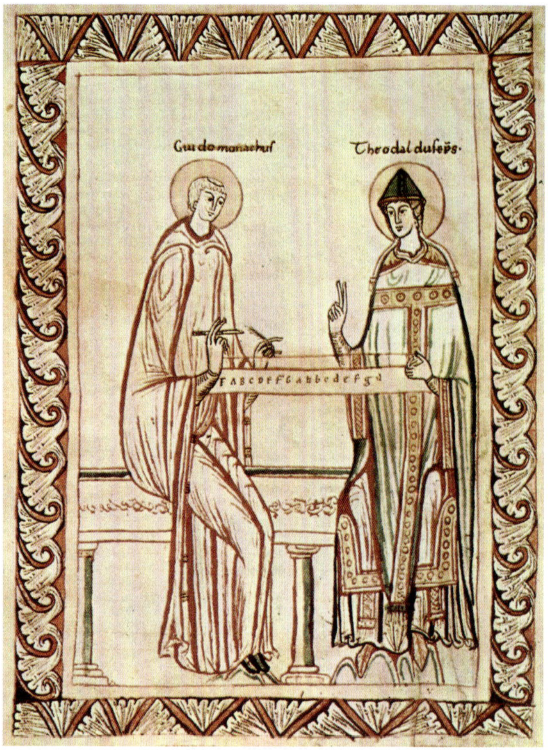

11. *Guido of Arezzo Explaining His Musical Notation*. Österreichische Nationalbibliothek, Vienna (E 2570–D, Cod. 51, fol. 35)

Metz, the priestly team directing the work in about the year 820 "labored and sweated over this project . . . to collect out of various books verses suitable to the responsories that we and many others cherish in the night office."[41]

An eleventh-century Italian breviary, drawing on the writings of Isidore of Seville, underlined the importance of the historical authority of composing and singing hymns, tracing its roots from biblical times through Saint Ambrose: "First the prophet David is known to have composed and sung hymns, then the other prophets, and afterwards, the three boys placed in the furnace, every creature having been called together, singing a hymn to the creator of all things." The text refers to hymns as "useful things for moving a pious soul, inflaming it with the effect of divine delight."[42]

Thus although psalmody was rooted in Jewish tradition, it was through the liturgy of the Christian majority population that the practice continued to develop in the Middle Ages. Among the

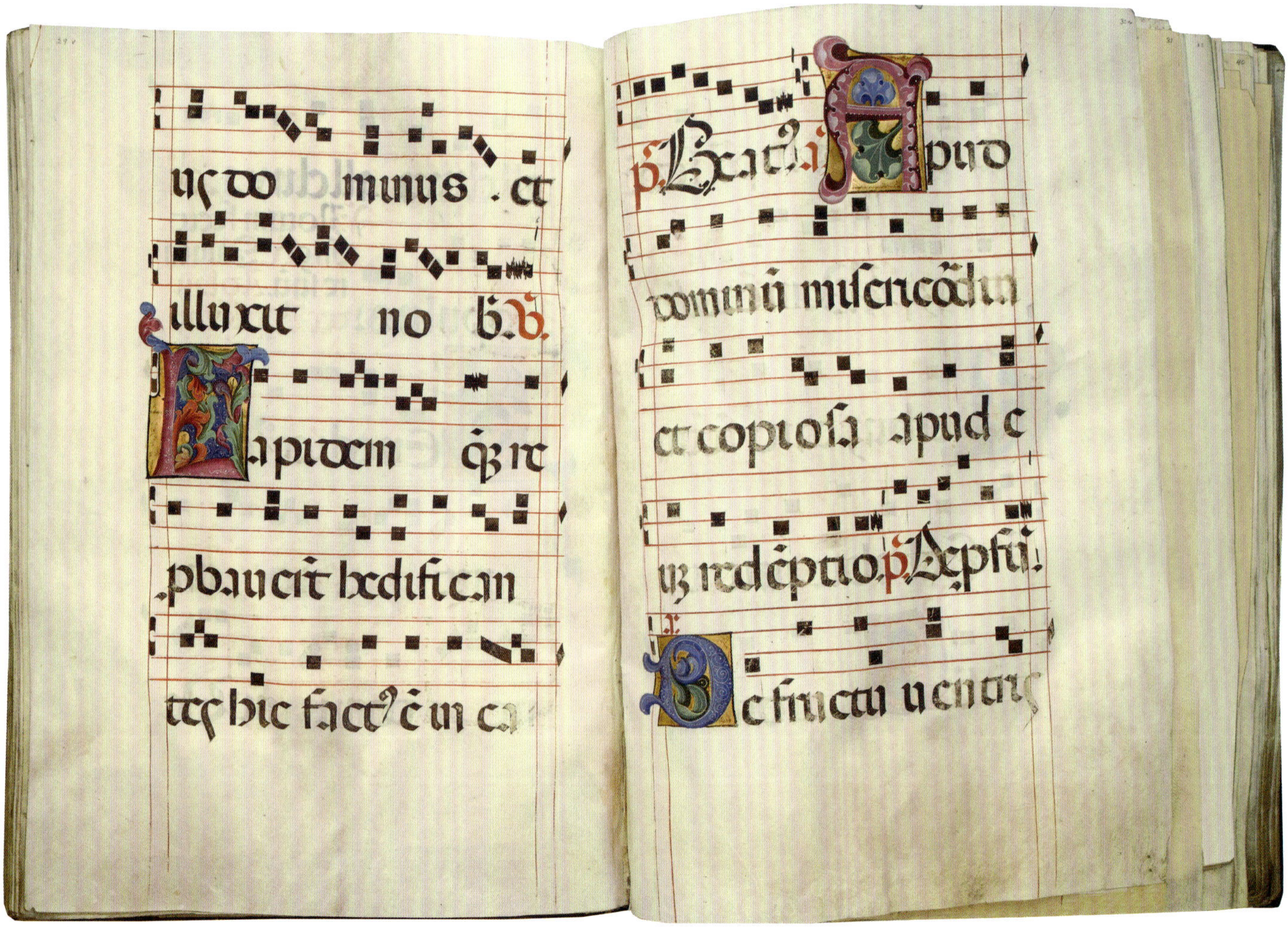

12. Belbello da Pavia (active ca. 1420–70) and collaborators. Antiphonary created for the Benedictine monastery of San Giorgio Maggiore, Venice. Lombardy, ca. 1467–70. Tempera, gold, and ink on parchment; each folio 22 ⅛ x 16 ⅛ in. (56.2 x 41 cm). The Metropolitan Museum of Art, Gift of Robert Lehman, 1960 (60.165)

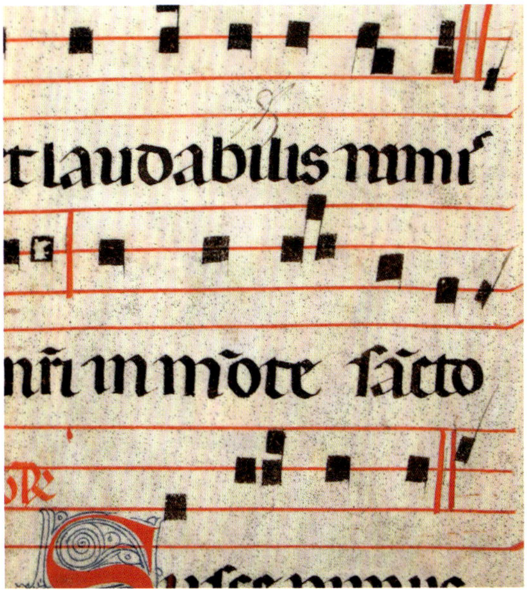

13. Detail of verso of fig. 69

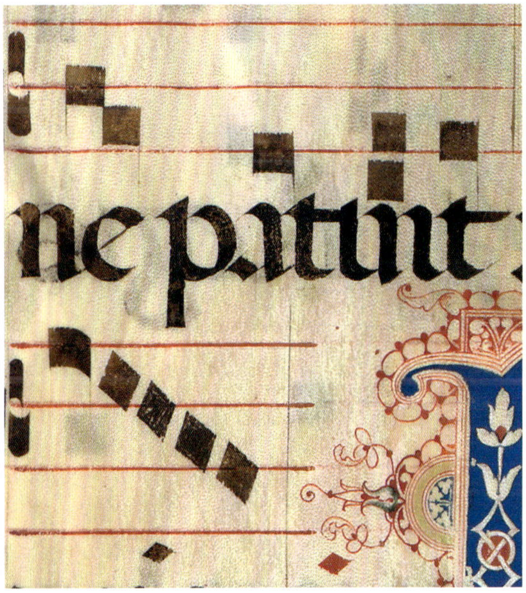

14. Detail of verso of fig. 30

thousands of centuries-old manuscripts found in the *genizah*, or storeroom, of the Ben Ezra Synagogue in Old Cairo is a musical text written by Obadiah, a Christian monk who converted to Judaism in 1102. The text, written on Egyptian papyrus, is a eulogy on Moses penned in Hebrew, but the music is recorded in a system of notation used by Christians in Italy in the twelfth and thirteenth centuries. Obadiah had adapted Gregorian chant to Hebrew poetry, bringing the melodies of Christian tradition to his new faith.[43]

### Musical Notation

***Recognize with how great care the neumes are arranged***

The argument in favor of systematizing musical notation was continued in the eleventh century by Guido of Arezzo, a town located southeast of Florence in the diocese of Tuscany. Concerned about boys "who receive terrible whippings because of their ignorance of psalms and ordinary learning,"[44] Guido (fig. 11) devised a system that allowed choir members to sing "correctly by themselves without a teacher, which thing any intelligent and diligent [person] will be able to do easily with the help of God." To accomplish this, singers "should strive to recognize with how great care the neumes are arranged." As Guido explained in his treatise (some seventy manuscripts of which have survived), in his system "pitches are so arranged that each sound, howsoever much it is repeated in a chant, is always found in one and the same row. In order that you can better distinguish these rows, lines are drawn closely, and they make some rows of pitches on the lines themselves, some between the lines, that is, in the space between the lines. Thus, however many sounds there are on one line or on one space, they all sound similarly."[45] The format he advocated lies at the heart of the modern practice of musical notation.

Not surprisingly, Guido of Arezzo's system of staff notation was first adopted in many parts of the Italian peninsula. The musical staff subsequently adopted for church choirs—and the one seen consistently in the Metropolitan's collection of choral manuscripts—consists of four lines rather than the modern five, with the curiously square neumes (the medieval antecedents of notes) set either on the lines or in the spaces. Where two square neumes are vertically aligned, the lower one is to be sung first, followed by the upper. Simple letters are used as clefs to indicate the location of a tone on a given staff. For example, a two-part mark representing a lower-case letter C indicates the location of the note we now call middle C. This can be seen along the left margin of the left-hand page of an antiphonary made for the monastery of San Giorgio Maggiore in Venice in the fifteenth century (fig. 12). The three-part symbol resembling a bracket or angular three-leaf clover that appears on the staves on the right-hand page of the same manuscript is an F, the tone five scale steps below C. So regularized was the system of scoring and notating the parchment for a given musical manuscript that the height of the staves and the distance between them can be used today to help confirm whether isolated leaves or cuttings come from the same

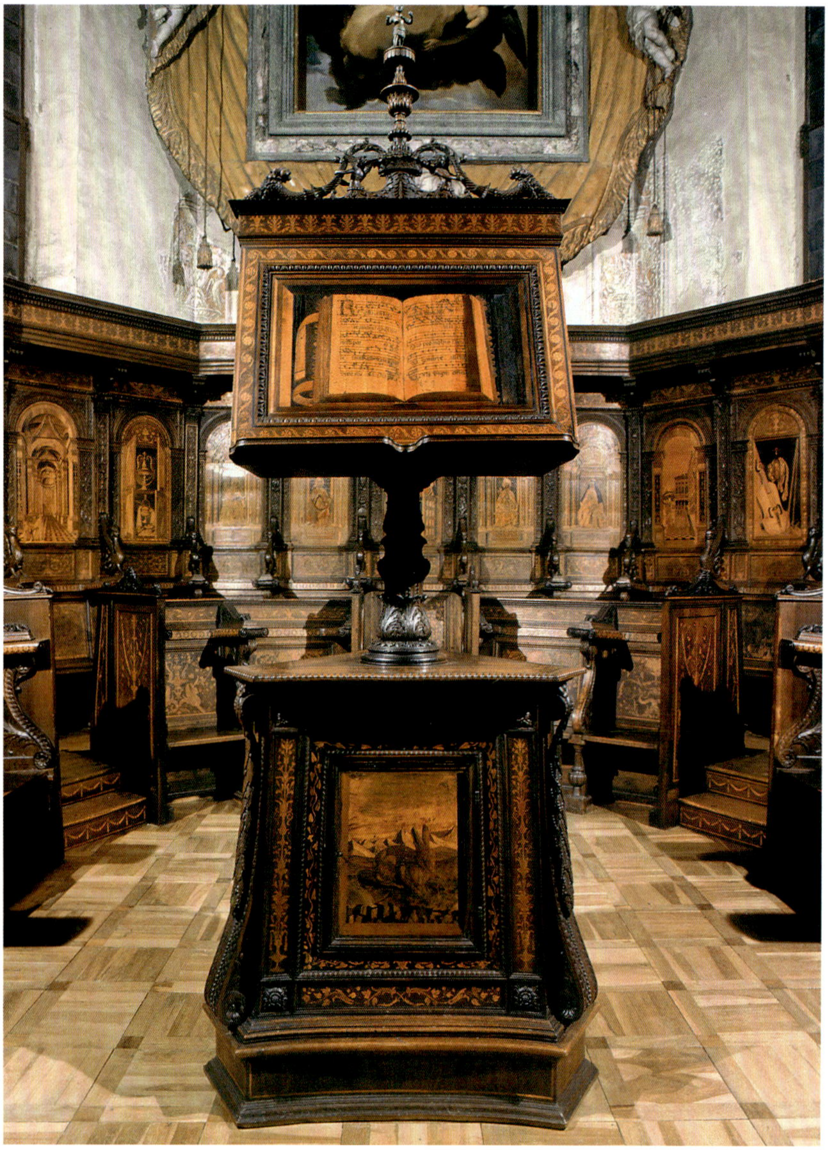

15. Fra Giovanni da Verona. Choral lectern from the Olivetan monastery of Santa Maria in Organo, Verona, 1500–1501. Intarsia, h. 10 ft. ½ in. (3.06 m)

parent manuscript. In general, the staff heights of Italian choral manuscripts increased from the fourteenth to the sixteenth century. In a late thirteenth-century cutting in the Metropolitan's collection (fig. 13), for example, the staves are 1¼ inches high, while in a fragment from a sixteenth-century manuscript (fig. 14) they measure 2⅛ inches.

The development of musical notation to indicate pitch had a profound impact on the creation of musical manuscripts and, ultimately, on their illumination. To accommodate Guido of Arezzo's staff notation the space between lines of text in a choral manuscript needed to be much greater. Then too, manuscripts had to be large enough to allow a group to sing from a shared book and sturdy enough to withstand turning during regular use. Illuminations typically show a handful of singing monks (see figs. 10, 43), but this may simply be a shorthand artistic convention. Between thirty and forty clergy participated in the exceptionally large choir at Siena Cathedral during the fifteenth century; in monasteries, convents, cathedrals, and even the papal chapel, smaller groups of singers young and old gathered around large wooden lecterns on which the choir books were placed (fig. 15; see fig. 43). Of course the enormous scale was not uniquely dependent on function; ostentation sometimes played a role as well, and very large lecterns served as a means of exhibiting the paintings in large and important choir books. This was the case with the ensemble commissioned with the support of public funds for Florence Cathedral in the fifteenth century.[46]

## Types of Musical Manuscripts

***Through all the choir, one voice, one measure ran, that perfect seem'd the concord of their song***

From the late thirteenth century decorated choral manuscripts were in increasingly widespread use in Western Europe, in large part as a result of the rapid growth of monastic communities. Most of the surviving illuminated manuscripts with musical notation are either graduals or antiphonaries (antiphoners). (Medieval references and scholars do not always distinguish between the two, either because they had not yet been separated into distinct volumes or because "antiphonary" has been adopted as a generic term for a choir book.) A gradual contains text and music sung by the choir during the celebration of the Mass (see fig. 16), the sacramental ceremony based on Jesus' instructions to his apostles at the Last Supper. The earliest graduals with musical notation date to the late ninth or early tenth century.[47] The antiphonary contains text and music sung during the celebration of the Divine Office, a daily cycle of prayers recited at set times of morning, noon, evening, and night.

The texts of the two types of services are sometimes intermingled in a single volume. The table of contents of the finely painted but relatively small Blumenthal choir book, for example (fig. 17), shows that the volume covers the feasts from Christmas through Pentecost and includes the sung portions of masses for saints according to their general type: martyrs, confessors, and virgin saints. In addition, it includes offices (prayer services) of the Virgin. Except during the twelve days of Christmas, the book has no special sung responses for particular saints; nor does it include texts for Advent, the four weeks preceding Christmas. Those texts, and the ones for the feasts that fall after Pentecost, the nearly half a year from spring to November, may have been in separate volumes.

In the eighth century, at the time of Charlemagne, the gradual already comprised about 560 elements, including 70 introits.[48] Introits mark the entrance into the sanctuary of the priest who will be celebrating the Mass. The text of the introit is often, but not exclusively, based on the opening verse of a psalm. As the choral equivalent of the beginning of a new chapter in a book, the introit is the musical element of the Mass most often illustrated with figural decoration in musical manuscripts. On single pages and cuttings the red letters of the word "Introit" or its abbreviation are sometimes recognizable. (See

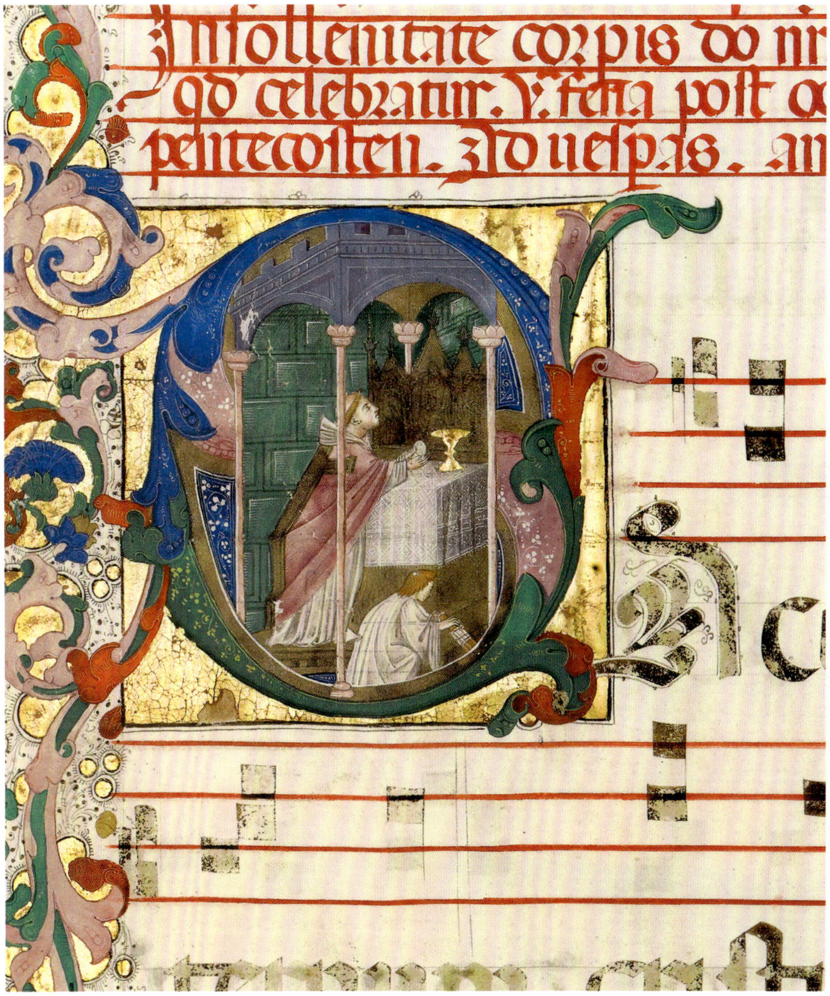

16. Master of the Riccardiana Lactantius. Leaf from a Benedictine antiphonary with *The Celebration of a Mass in an Initial S* (detail). Florence, second half of 15th century. Tempera, gold, and ink on parchment; leaf 21 9/16 x 16 1/8 in. (54.7 x 40.9 cm). The Metropolitan Museum of Art, Gift of Louis L. Lorillard, 1896, transferred from the Library (96.32.8). See also frontispiece, page 2

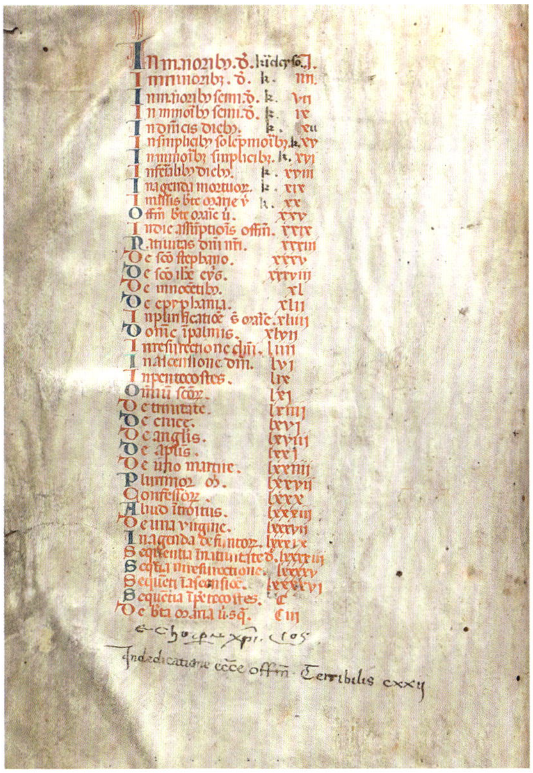

17. Leaf from a gradual with its table of contents. Florence, ca. 1310–15. Tempera and ink on parchment; gradual 13 3/8 x 9 7/8 x 2 5/8 in. (34.1 x 25 x 6.8 cm). The Metropolitan Museum of Art, Gift of George Blumenthal, 1941 (41.100.191)

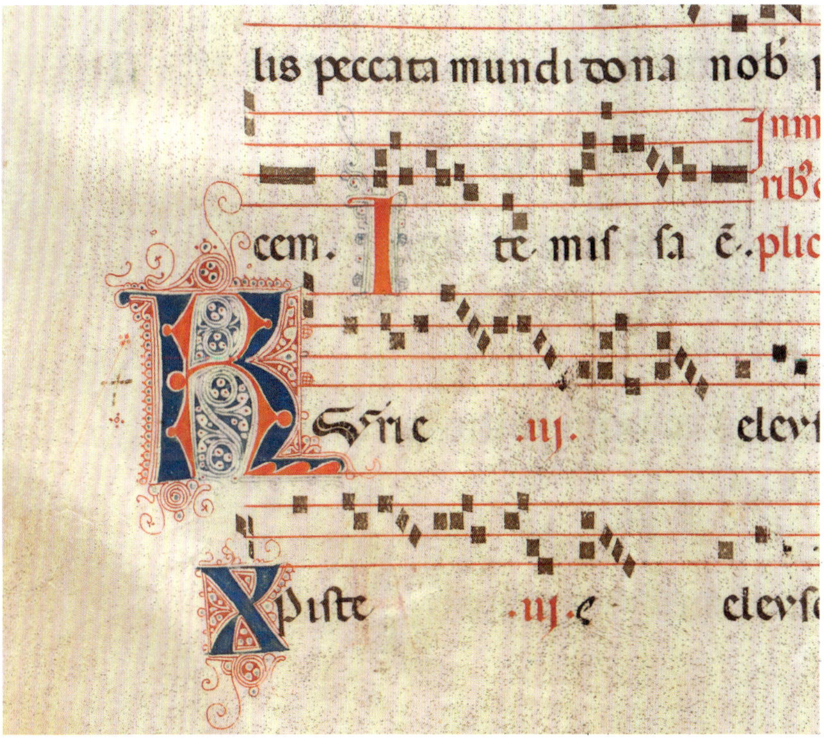


18. Leaf in the same gradual as fig. 17 with *Kyrie eleison* (detail)

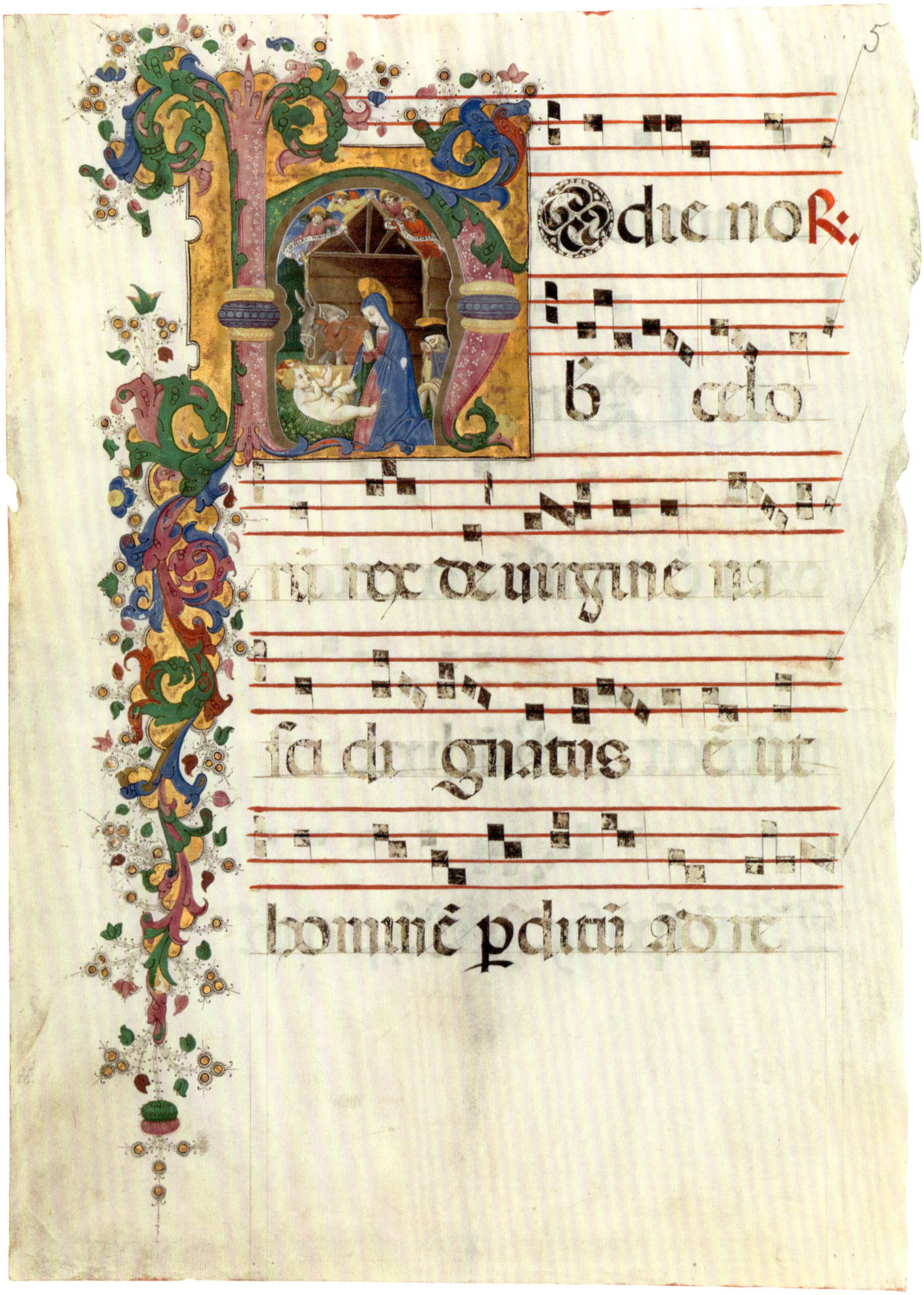

19. Master of the Riccardiana Lactantius. Leaf from a Benedictine antiphonary with *The Nativity in an Initial H.* Florence, second half of 15th century. Tempera, gold, and ink on parchment; 21⅞ x 15⅞ in. (55.5 x 40.3 cm). The Metropolitan Museum of Art, Gift of Louis L. Lorillard, 1896, transferred from the Library (96.32.5)

figs. 54 and 55, two pages from the same manuscript with "Introit" abbreviated on one and written in full on the other.) Texts recited at almost every Mass, like a *Kyrie eleison,* a prayer for God's mercy, often have decorated but not figural initials (see fig. 18).

Parts of a gradual may be bound together by the types of feasts. Feasts with a fixed date, like Christmas, might be grouped in a book, or feasts for saints' days might be bound together in a Sanctorale (sometimes called the Sanctoral Cycle) and moveable feasts like Easter and Pentecost in a Temporale (sometimes called the Temporal Cycle). Text and music for saints who do not have their own distinct readings, or Propers, might be grouped in a Communale (sometimes called the Common of Saints). Consequently, graduals are often composed of a number of volumes. The cathedral of Siena, for example, ordered a gradual in twelve volumes in 1457, and a second ensemble of twelve books was created from 1462 to 1466.[49]

The prayers necessary for singing the Divine Office, the daily cycle of monastic devotions, came to be contained in a choir book, or set of choir books, referred to in modern terminology as an antiphonary. The particular hours of the day at which prayers are sung vary according to the monastic order; the times cited here are those codified by Saint Benedict in the sixth century. Text and music for the daily prayer cycles in an antiphonary begin with Matins, from *matutinus*, Latin for "early in the morning." (The term is somewhat euphemistic, as Saint Benedict directed that Matins be intoned at about 3:00 a.m.) The service for Matins includes an introduction and one to three (depending on the feast and the practice of the particular monastic community) nocturns, each composed of several psalms, antiphons that introduce and conclude each psalm, and sung responsories that complement biblical readings. Matins is followed by Lauds ("Praises") as the sky brightens before sunrise. The Little Hours follow through the day (Prime at 6:00, Terce at 9:00, Sext at noon, None at 3:00 p.m.). Vespers ("Evening") is sung at twilight, just as the lamps are lit. The service of Vespers echoes Lauds, though sometimes with less variety in the antiphons. Some feasts are marked by two Vespers services, one, called the Vigil or First Vespers, on the evening before and another, called Second Vespers, on the appointed day. A simpler service of Compline, from the Latin for "completed," marks the end of day. (The day's principal Mass, for which the sung parts are recorded in the gradual, would usually be celebrated between Terce and Sext.)

Because it contained so many daily services per year and so many chants per service, a complete medieval antiphonary included as many as 1,500 antiphons.[50] Antiphonaries for use by Benedictine, Cistercian, and Carthusian monks contained even more antiphons than those compiled for ordinary clergy and the mendicant orders, notably the Franciscans, Dominicans, and Augustinians. Consequently, antiphonaries were often divided into even more volumes than graduals, arranged either according to the calendar year or by time of day, with antiphons for daytime use in a Diurnale. To save space the psalms and canticles for a particular feast are summarily indicated but rarely transcribed; instead, they are gathered together in a supplement.[51]

That individual pages or cuttings came from an antiphonary can often be recognized by the many sometimes complicated rubrics, or notations in red

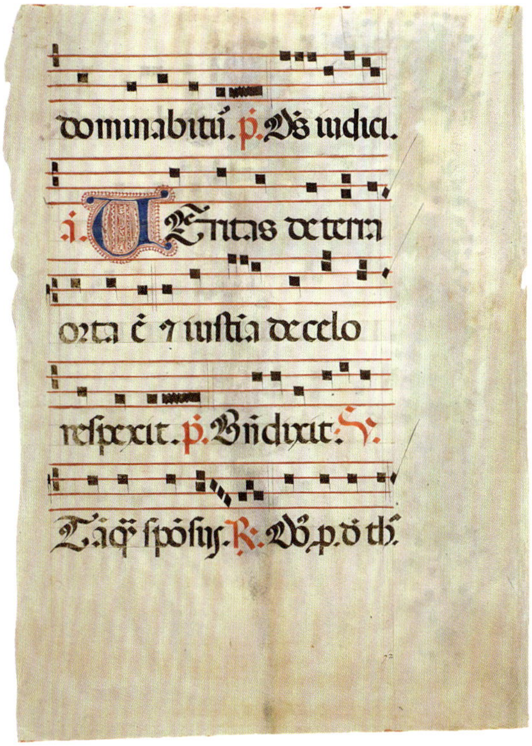

20. Verso of fig. 19

ink, that indicate verses ("V"), responses ("R"), and psalms ("P") (see figs. 19, 20) or, though they are not exclusive to antiphonaries, by the appearance of the letters *EUOUAE* (fig. 21), a mnemonic formed from the vowels in the Latin "seculorum. Amen," the closing words of the *Gloria Patri*, the doxology sung at the end of the chants, before the final repetition of the opening antiphon. (The full text in Latin, "Gloria Patri, et Filio, et Spiritui Sancto, Sicut erat in principio, et nunc, et semper, et in secula seculorum. Amen," translates as "Glory be to the Father, and to the Son, and to the Holy Spirit. As it was in the beginning, is now, and ever shall be, world without end. Amen.")

From the time of Charlemagne on, portions of the Gregorian repertory were shared by monastic communities across Europe. Some of the chants must have been as familiar as Christmas carols are today. One of the most frequently illuminated hymns in medieval choral manuscripts (but sadly missing from the Metropolitan's collection) is the gradual introit for Christmas Day that begins *Puer natus est*, the opening words familiar to us in the English of Handel's *Messiah*: "For unto us a child is born" (see fig. 22).

The writings of Dante testify to the widespread familiarity of certain chants in the fourteenth century. The *Divine Comedy* makes repeated references

21. Leaf in the Benedictine antiphonary shown in fig. 12 with a chant ending with the letters *EUOUAE*

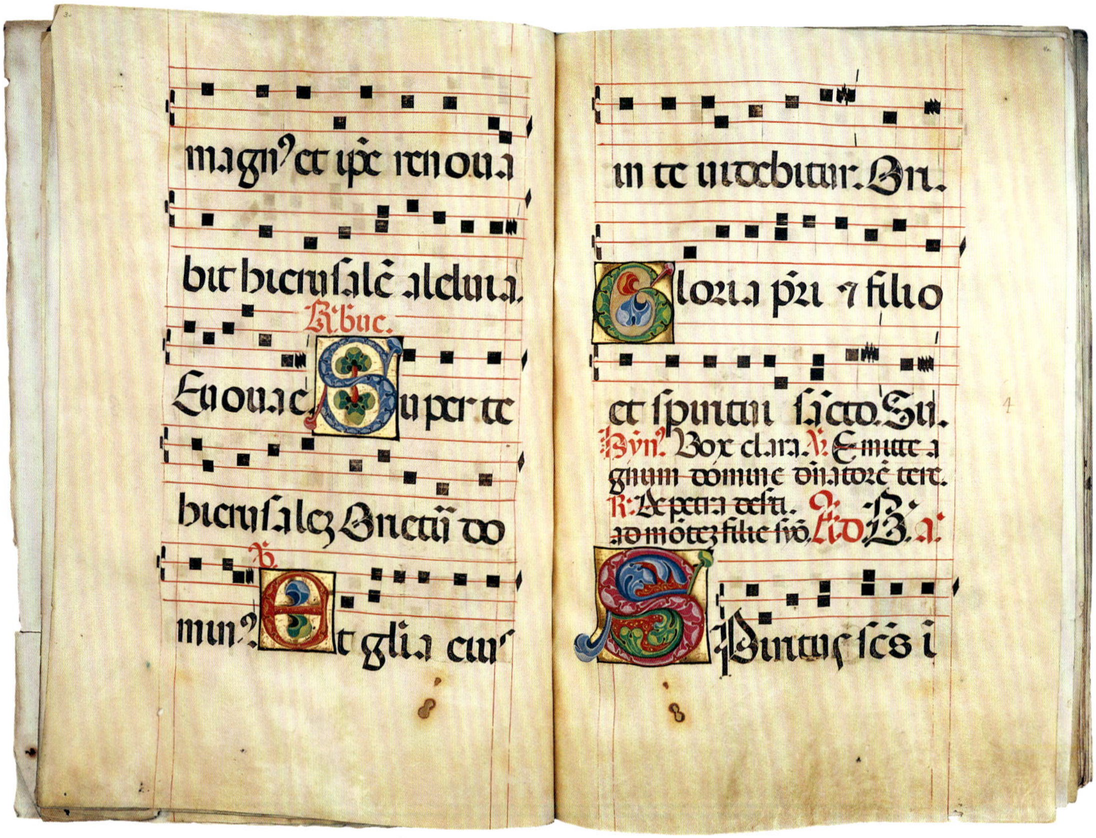

to singing and to specific chants. Chants allowed Dante to "go outside himself"; they moved him to tears. Clearly his readers were meant to be familiar with hymns like "Te lucis ante terminum" (Before the End of Light), sung at Compline; "Te Deum laudamus" (We Praise You, O God); "In te, Domine, speravi" (In You God, Have I Hoped), which caused the poet to cry; and "Asperges me" (Cleanse Me), which he found beyond description.[52] The singing of the *Agnus Dei* (Lamb of God) left Dante rhapsodic: "Through all the choir / One voice, one measure ran, that perfect seem'd / The concord of their song."[53]

Still today some Christian hymnals include verses that were first used in medieval choir books. These draw not only on a wide range of psalms and New Testament texts but also on the poetic words of medieval churchmen, notably Gregory the Great but also Saint Ambrose, bishop of Milan in the fourth century; Venantius Fortunatus, the sixth-century author of the Easter hymns "Hail Thee, Festival Day" and "Welcome, Happy Morning"; Alcuin of York and Rabanus Maurus, both associated with the court of Charlemagne; and John of Damascus, who lived in the eighth century. Peter Abelard (1079–1153), Bernard of Clairvaux (1090–1153), and Saint Francis of Assisi (1182–1226) all have hymns associated with their names.

(opposite)
22. Don Silvestro dei Gherarducci (1339–1399). Leaf from a gradual with *The Nativity and the Annunciation to the Shepherds in an Initial P.* Florence, 1392–99. From the choir books created for the Camaldolese monastery of Santa Maria degli Angeli, Florence. Tempera, gold, and ink on parchment; 23 ¼ x 15 ¾ in. (59 x 40 cm). The Pierpont Morgan Library, New York, Gift of J. P. Morgan (1867–1943), 1924 (MS M.653.1)

## The Illumination of the Choir Book

***The leisure of a cloister often produced Artists of great ability in this way***

In the nineteenth century the English collector William Ottley observed, somewhat romantically, that he was sure "that the leisure of a cloister often produced Artists of great ability in this way."[54] But the documentary evidence of monastic production of choir books paints a picture of frenetic industry rather than creative leisure. Over the course of the Middle Ages new choir books were produced on a fairly regular basis to accommodate changes in the service, the addition of feasts for new saints and newly established holidays, the reformation of monasteries by groups like the Cistercians and Camaldolese, the creation of entirely new monastic orders and the formulation of their rules, and the growth of monastic orders.

Following its establishment in 1205, the Dominican order focused on the regulation of its liturgy, which required standardized liturgical manuscripts.[55]

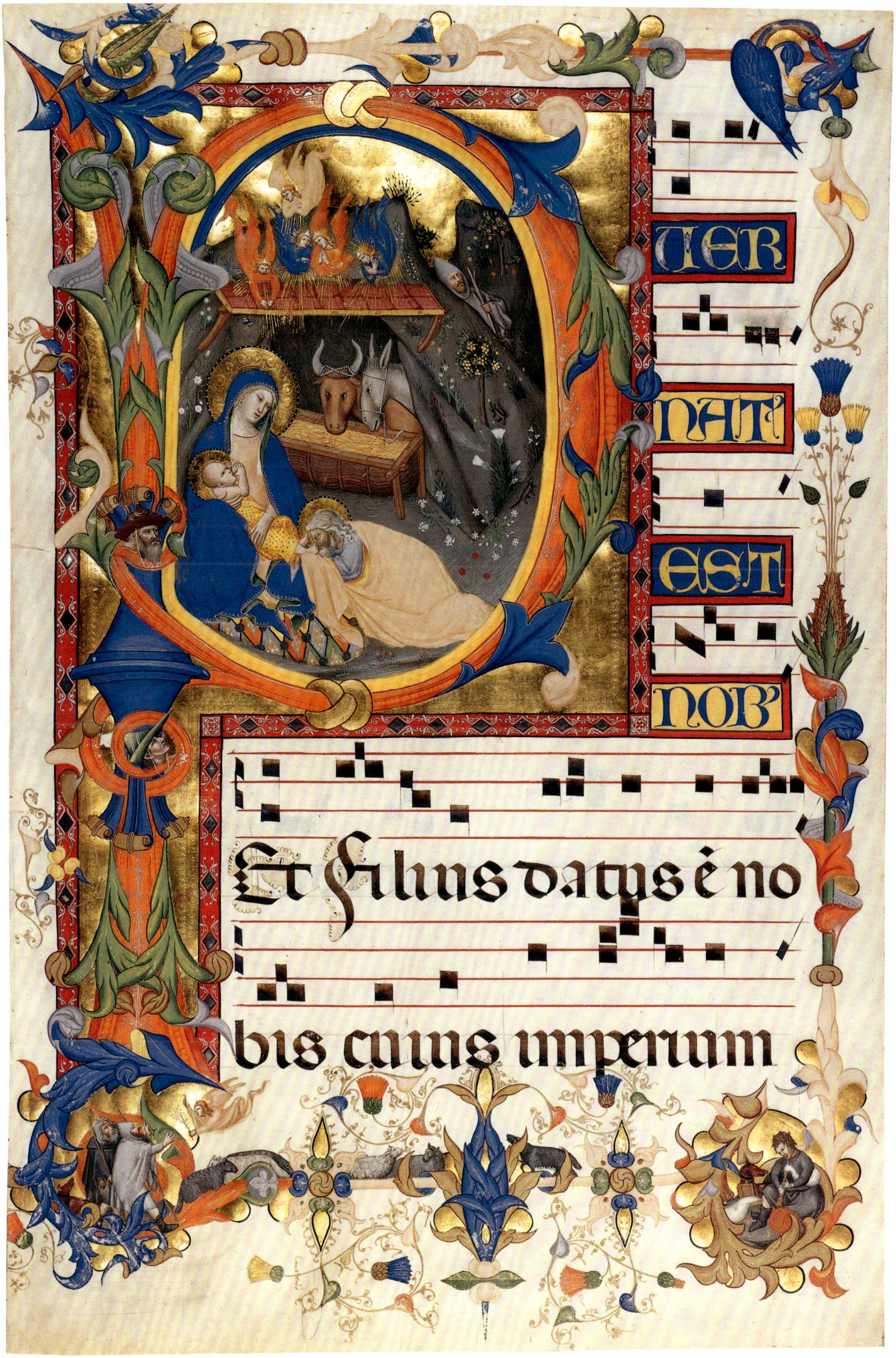
UER
NAT'
EST
NOB'
Et filius datus ē no
bis cuius imperium

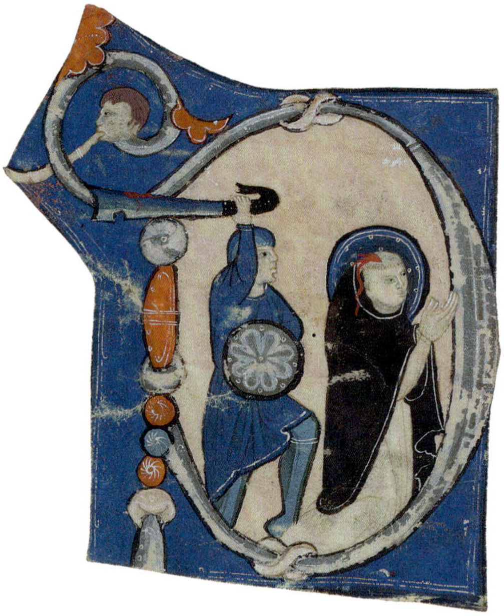

23. *Initial P with the Martyrdom of Saint Peter Martyr.* Bologna, second half of 13th century. From a Dominican antiphonary. Tempera and ink on parchment; 3 1/8 x 2 13/16 in. (7.9 x 7.1 cm). The Metropolitan Museum of Art, Gift of Bashford Dean, 1923 (23.21.2)

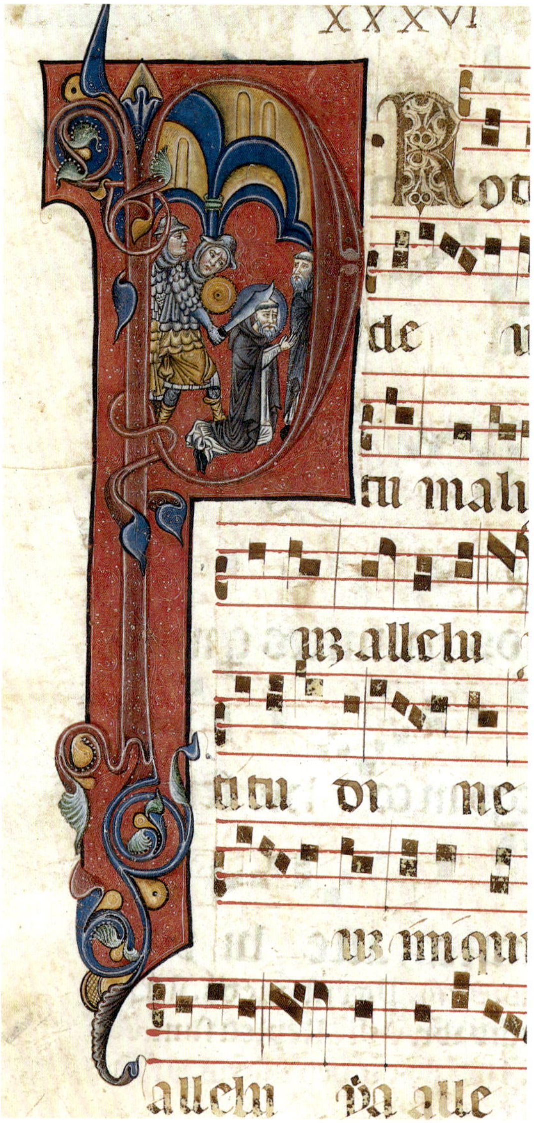

24. Leaf from a Dominican gradual with *The Martyrdom of Saint Peter Martyr in an Initial P* (detail). Southern Italy, probably Naples, second half of 13th century. Tempera and ink on parchment; leaf 18 3/4 x 13 1/4 in. (47.5 x 33.5 cm). The Metropolitan Museum of Art, Purchase, Ronald R. Atkins, James Marrow, Elaine Rosenberg, and R. R. Atkins Foundation Gifts, 2005 (2005.273)

Each Dominican community was to provide books for the community's use, including paired or multiple copies when necessary to ensure that all the friars could see the texts from their choir stalls.[56] Dominican records indicate that the business of music was to be taken very seriously: in 1270 the provincial chapter in Milan issued instructions that the teaching of chant be improved, and in 1272 it decreed that recalcitrant priors were to be punished with a restricted diet of bread and water for two days.[57]

Though he was canonized just three years earlier, in 1253 (within a fortnight of his martyrdom), Saint Peter Martyr appears in the Dominican liturgy authorized in 1256. An early image of the saint's martyrdom enclosed in a letter P (fig. 23), with its predominant red and blue palette and sturdy squat figures, is characteristic of manuscript illumination at Bologna, the foremost center of the Dominican order in Italy. As he kneels calmly in prayer, Peter is attacked from behind by an evil knight and suffers a mortal wound to the head. The scene conforms to the formula that had been adopted for the martyrdom of Thomas Becket, creating a kind of visual equivalent to the use, musically, of a common antiphon for saints of the same type. While ultimately the illustration depends on long-established depictions of the stoning of Saint Stephen, the similarity to the Becket scene becomes more explicit in a second illumination in the Metropolitan's collection (fig. 24). Like Becket's martyrdom in Canterbury Cathedral, the event is set in a church interior, even though the Dominican Peter Martyr was killed outdoors. The rounded arches of the space echo the form of the letter P. In an illumination of the translation, or ceremonial moving, of the revered body of Saint Dominic (fig. 25), the same artist used an elongated trefoil arch that better conforms to the shape of a tall letter I.

The Franciscan order was founded four years after the Dominican, in 1209. A liturgical office in honor of Saint Francis of Assisi was composed in 1231–32, soon after the translation of the saint's relics. At Christmas in 1252, according to legend, Saint Clare had a vision of the celebration of Mass at Assisi during which an office in honor of Saint Francis was sung by the brothers to organ accompaniment. The church Clare saw in her dream was consecrated in May 1253, and within a lustrum its records show payments for new choral manuscripts.[58]

For the creation of new manuscripts the Franciscans at Rimini seem to have established a scriptorium near their church. In their instructions to the scribes who worked on choir books the order specified that the notes were to be square and the lettering open and clear.[59] Legibility of the text was paramount.

Four cuttings in the Metropolitan Museum (figs. 26–29), two from an antiphonary and two from a gradual, were very likely part of an ensemble of choir books from a community of Franciscan observants, perhaps Santo Spirito at Ferrara.[60] They are part of a group of fragments that have been linked to the Ferrarese painter Cosmè Tura, whom Duke Borso d'Este named court painter in 1458. Among the brown-clad saints assembled for the Feast of All Saints in the scene on one of the Museum's cuttings (fig. 27) is John Capistrano (1385–1456), who in the 1420s was accused and then acquitted of heresy for working with Saint Bernardine to reform the Franciscan order.

The Olivetan order, founded in 1319, likewise required liturgical books for its communities, which numbered more than one hundred in Italy by the end of the sixteenth century. The first monastic constitutions for the order, drafted in 1445, included manuscript illumination among the work activities appropriate for monks.[61] Secular artists like Girolamo dai Libri also created manuscripts under contract for Olivetan houses. The monastery of Santa Maria in Organo in Verona became Olivetan in 1444; an illumination from a psalter it commissioned in 1501–2 (see fig. 10) shows singing monks in characteristic Olivetan white robes.[62] That distinctive clue made it possible to reconstruct the provenance of the image of David praying (fig. 7) that was cut from the same manuscript.

The spectacular choir books from the church of Santa Maria degli Angeli in Florence (see figs. 47, 59, 60) were begun by its monks, who belonged to

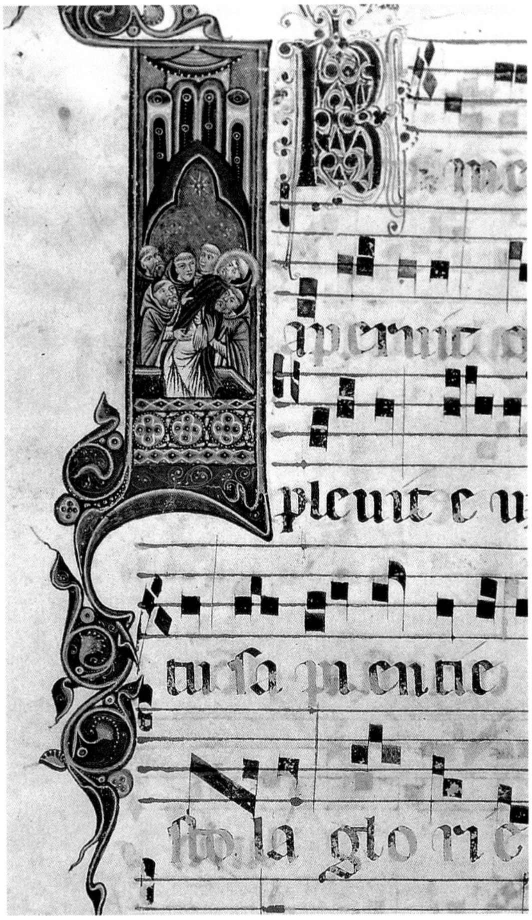

25. Leaf from a Dominican gradual with *The Translation of the Body of Saint Dominic in an Initial I* (detail). Bologna, second half of 13th century. Tempera and ink on parchment; leaf 18½ x 13½ in. (47 x 34.3 cm). Allen Memorial Art Museum, Oberlin College, Ohio, Gift of Robert Lehman, 1943 (43.10)

the Camaldolese order founded by Saint Romuald in the early eleventh century. Following the dictates of the order, the monks remained isolated for much of the day, usually eating their meals alone in their cells, but the community came together to celebrate the Divine Office by reciting the entire psalter each day. The Santa Maria degli Angeli choir books were as lavishly decorated as the monks' lifestyle was sober. According to Vasari, only the fact that they were for Camaldolese use dissuaded the Medici Pope Leo X from appropriating them for use at the Vatican.[63]

The Feast of Saint John Gualbert (985 or 995–1073), who founded the Vallombrosan order just before 1038, is included only in medieval choir books used by the order's monks. More than sixty Vallombrosan communities existed by the time Innocent III became pope in 1198, and by 1500 there were more than eighty in Tuscany alone. The scene on a leaf in the Metropolitan's collection for the first antiphon at Vespers of the Feast of Saint John Gualbert, celebrated on July 12 (fig. 30), conforms to the formula for presenting the saint's miracle that was established in the fourteenth

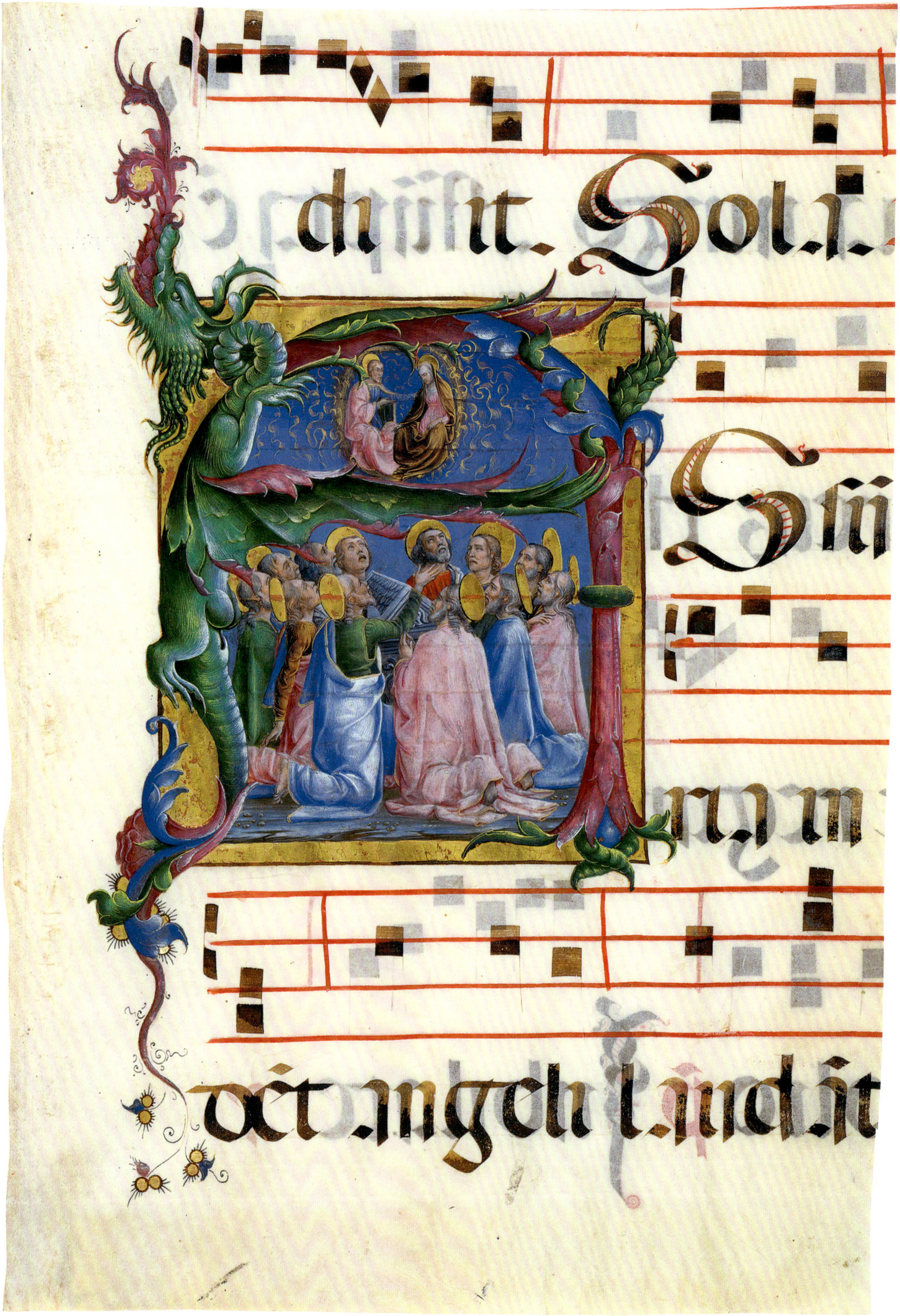

(opposite)
26. Attributed to Cosmè Tura (1430?–1495). *Initial A with the Assumption of the Virgin*. Ferrara, 1450–60. From a Franciscan antiphonary. Tempera, gold, and ink on parchment; 17 ¼ x 12 ⅛ in. (43.9 x 30.8 cm). The Metropolitan Museum of Art, Rogers Fund, 1911 (11.50.1)

27. Attributed to Cosmè Tura. *Initial V with All Saints*. Ferrara, 1450–60. From a Franciscan antiphonary. Tempera, gold, and ink on parchment; 14 ½ x 12 ⅛ in. (36.8 x 30.8 cm). The Metropolitan Museum of Art, Rogers Fund, 1911 (11.50.2)

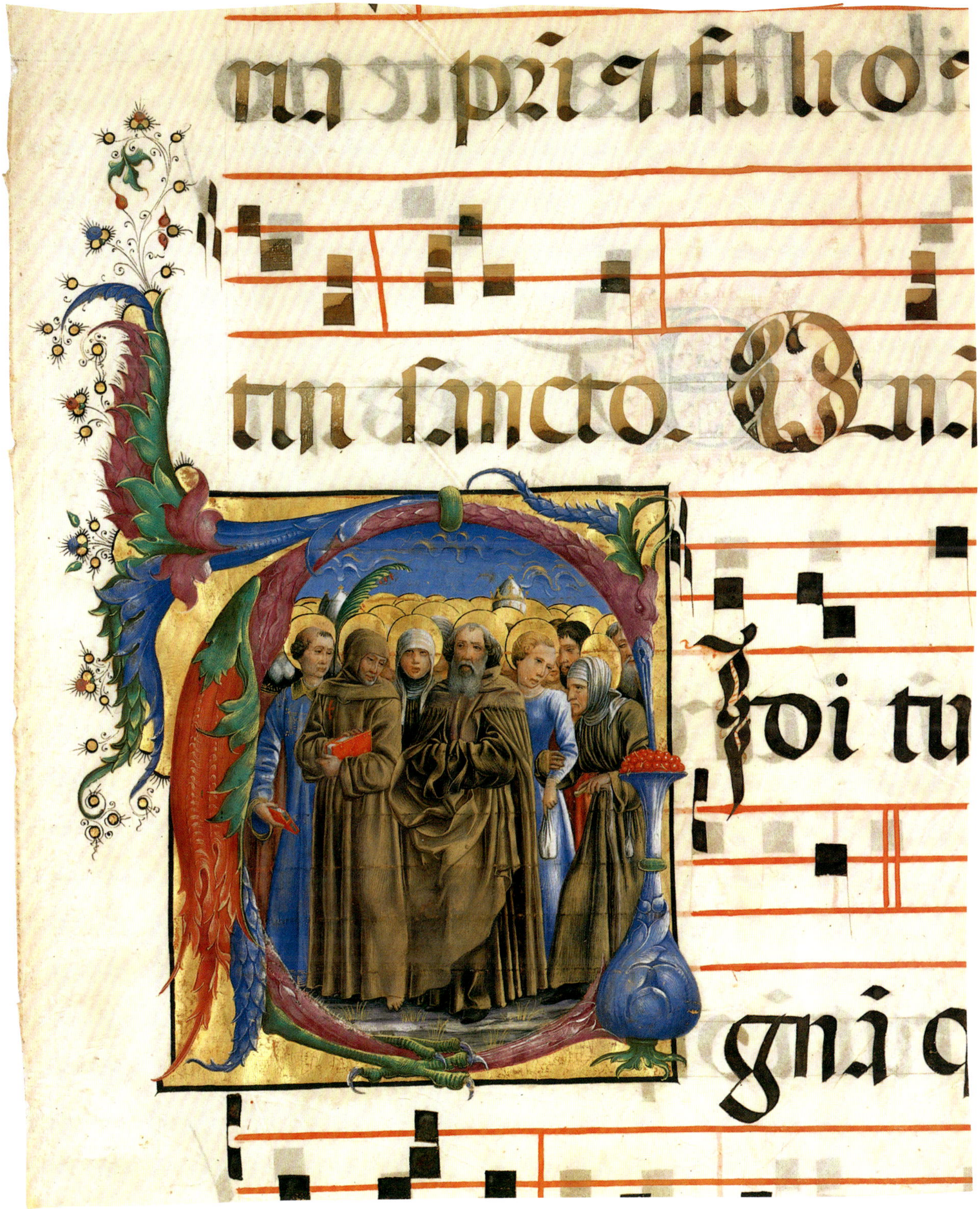

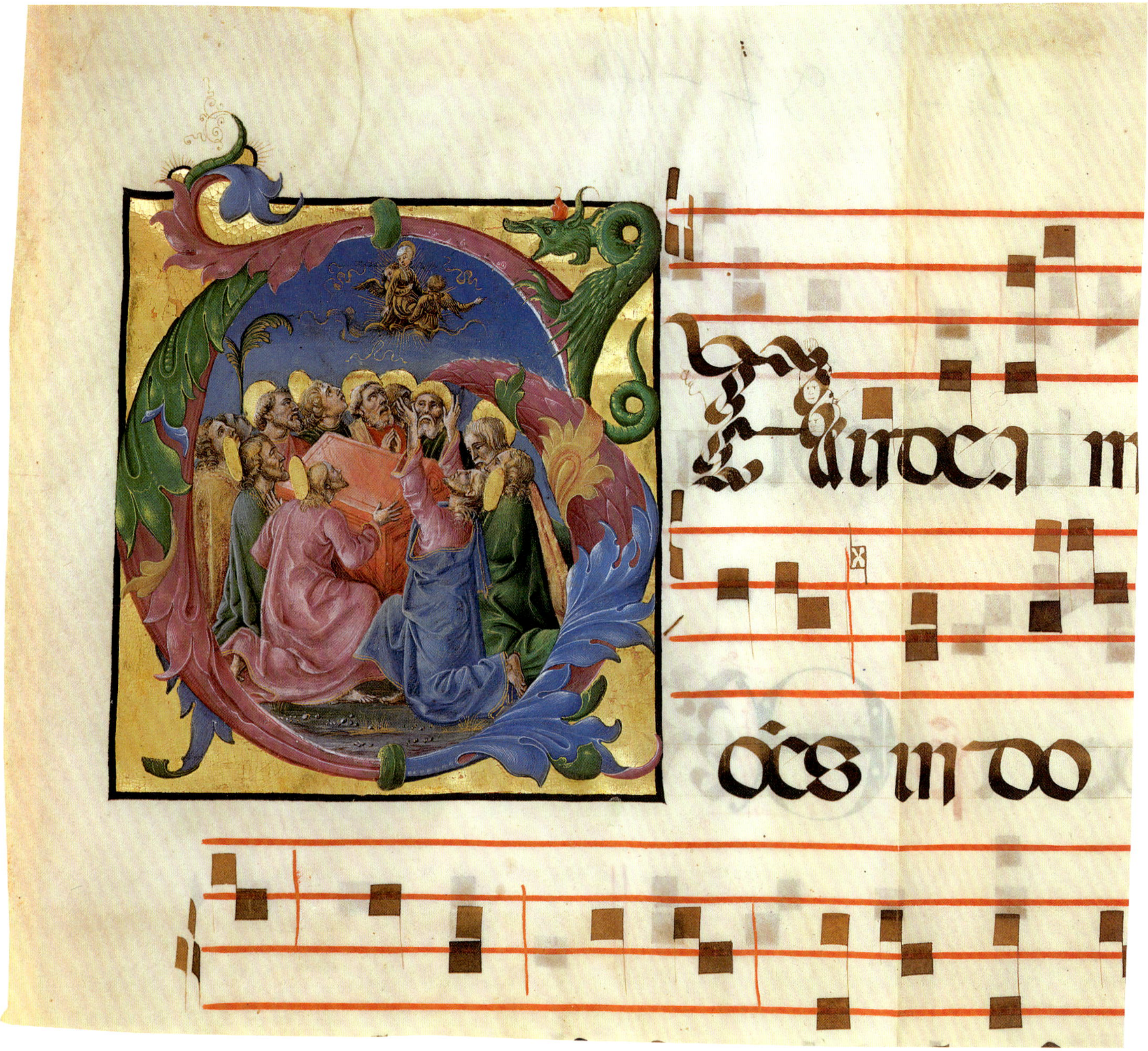

28. Attributed to Cosmè Tura. *Initial G with the Assumption of the Virgin*. Ferrara, 1450–60. From a Franciscan gradual. Tempera, gold, and ink on parchment; 12 ¼ x 13 ⅝ in. (31.2 x 34.5 cm). The Metropolitan Museum of Art, Rogers Fund, 1911 (11.50.3)

century, as exemplified by a painting attributed to Niccolò di Pietro Gerini (fig. 31), which in turn appears to have been based on an altarpiece by Giovanni del Biondo for the Franciscan church of Santa Croce in Florence. Following that convention, the artist who illuminated the Metropolitan's leaf, probably in Umbria in the early sixteenth century, telescoped two distinct moments into a single scene. As he was entering Florence one Good Friday accompanied by armed soldiers, having just been victorious in battle, John Gualbert, who was a member of the noble Visdomini family, came upon the man who had murdered his brother. Instead of killing him, when the man begged for forgiveness Gualbert pardoned him. Later, as Gualbert knelt in prayer in the church of San Miniato, the image of the crucified Christ bowed his head in approving recognition of his mercy. The space in the illumination is ambiguous: the architectural niche suggests a church interior or possibly a roadside chapel, but the saint and the sinner stand on green ground, the saint's horse appears at the left, and a sliver of sky is visible at either side of the altar. The antiphon tells the story in a rather militant tone that is reinforced by the attire of the saint, who carries a sword known as a falchion and

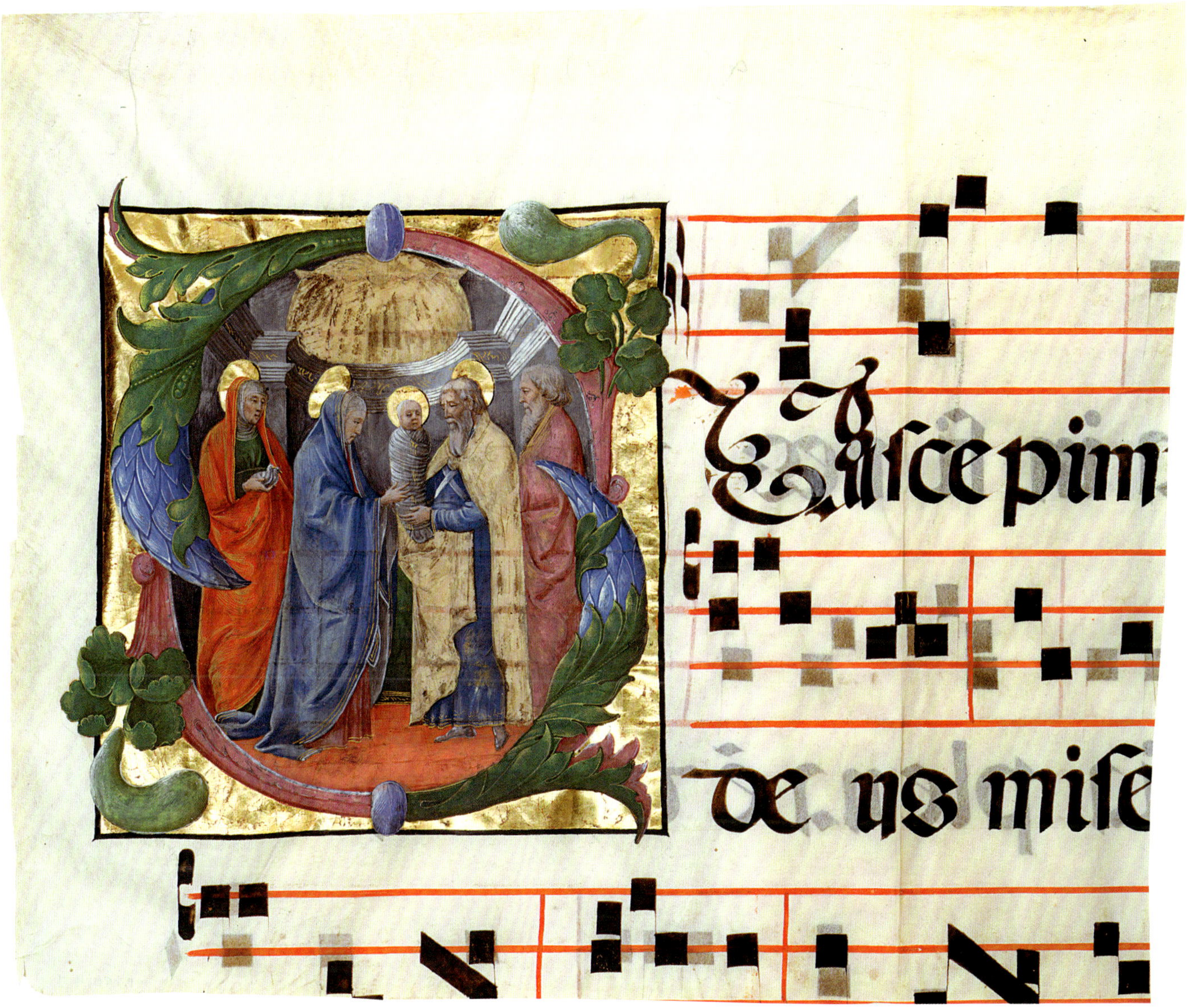

wears Italian-style armor with mail sleeves protruding over the arm defenses.[64] The horse, peeking out from the edge of the letter S, signifies both Gualbert's journey and his social status. The artist shows the letter S with a hollow center, as if it were a cut flower stem or blood vessel. A tau staff (so called because it assumes the form of a letter T), an emblem of the saint, appears in the border, as do intertwined letters S and T. Also in the border is an as yet unsolved clue to the original provenance of the leaf: the coat of arms of a bishop or abbot: *Azure a Lion rampant Argent impaling Gules a Cross (dimidiated) Argent.*[65]

Just as the holidays honored by particular orders could affect the illuminations in a choir book, so too could new holidays established universally. In 1389 Pope Urban VI decreed that the entire Church should celebrate the Feast of the Visitation of the Virgin Mary with her cousin Elizabeth, mother of John the Baptist. Communities in Italy that were loyal to the pope in Rome immediately embraced the feast, while churches loyal to the pope in Avignon lagged behind. The office for the feast was written by an English cardinal, Adam Easton. It is apparently Easton who appears in the central medallion at the bottom of a page in the Museum's collection

29. Attributed to Cosmè Tura. *Initial S with the Presentation in the Temple.* Ferrara, 1450–60. From a Franciscan gradual. Tempera, gold, and ink on parchment; 11 ¼ x 13 ½ in. (28.5 x 34.4 cm). The Metropolitan Museum of Art, Rogers Fund, 1911 (11.50.4)

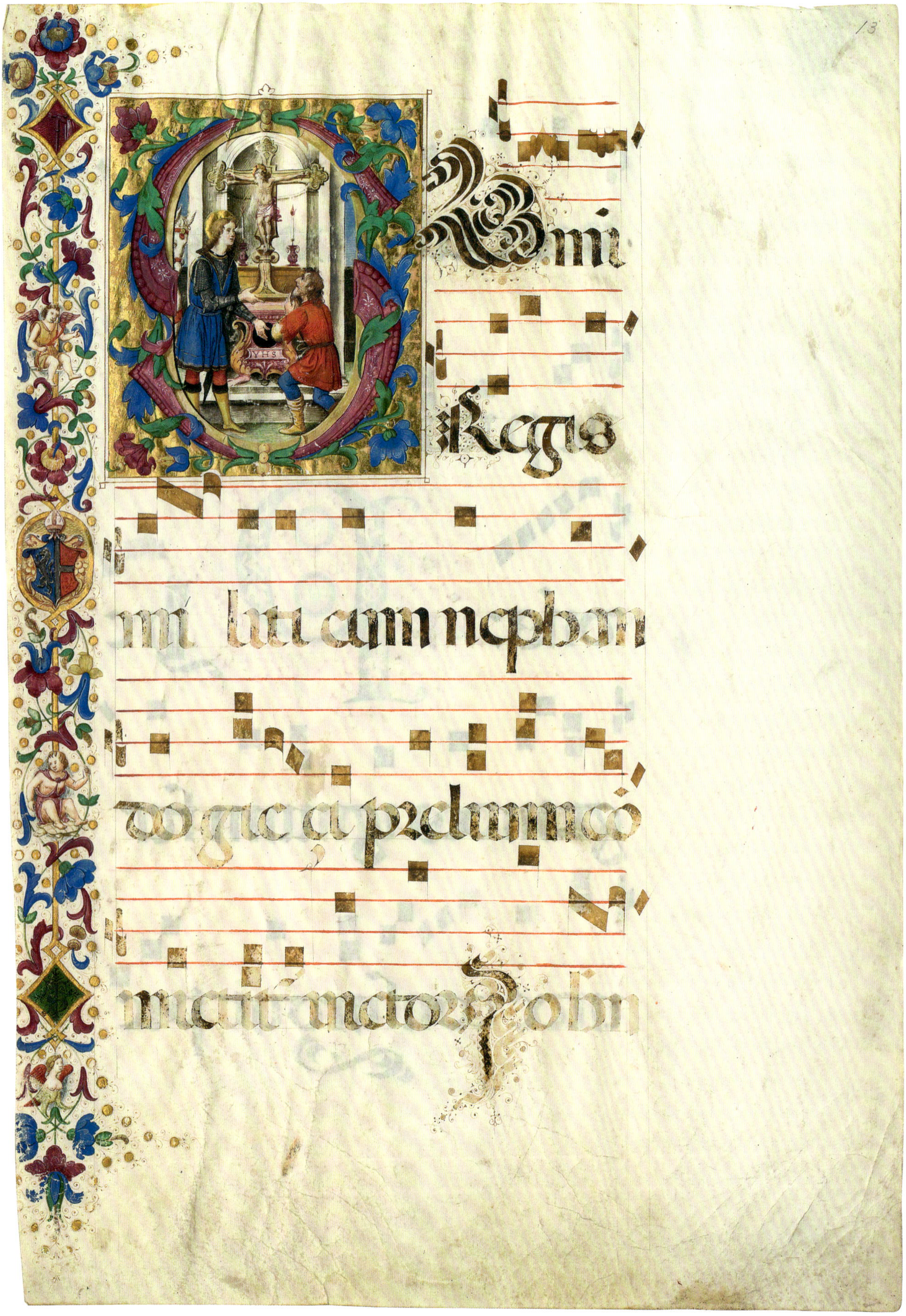
13
YHS
mi
Regis

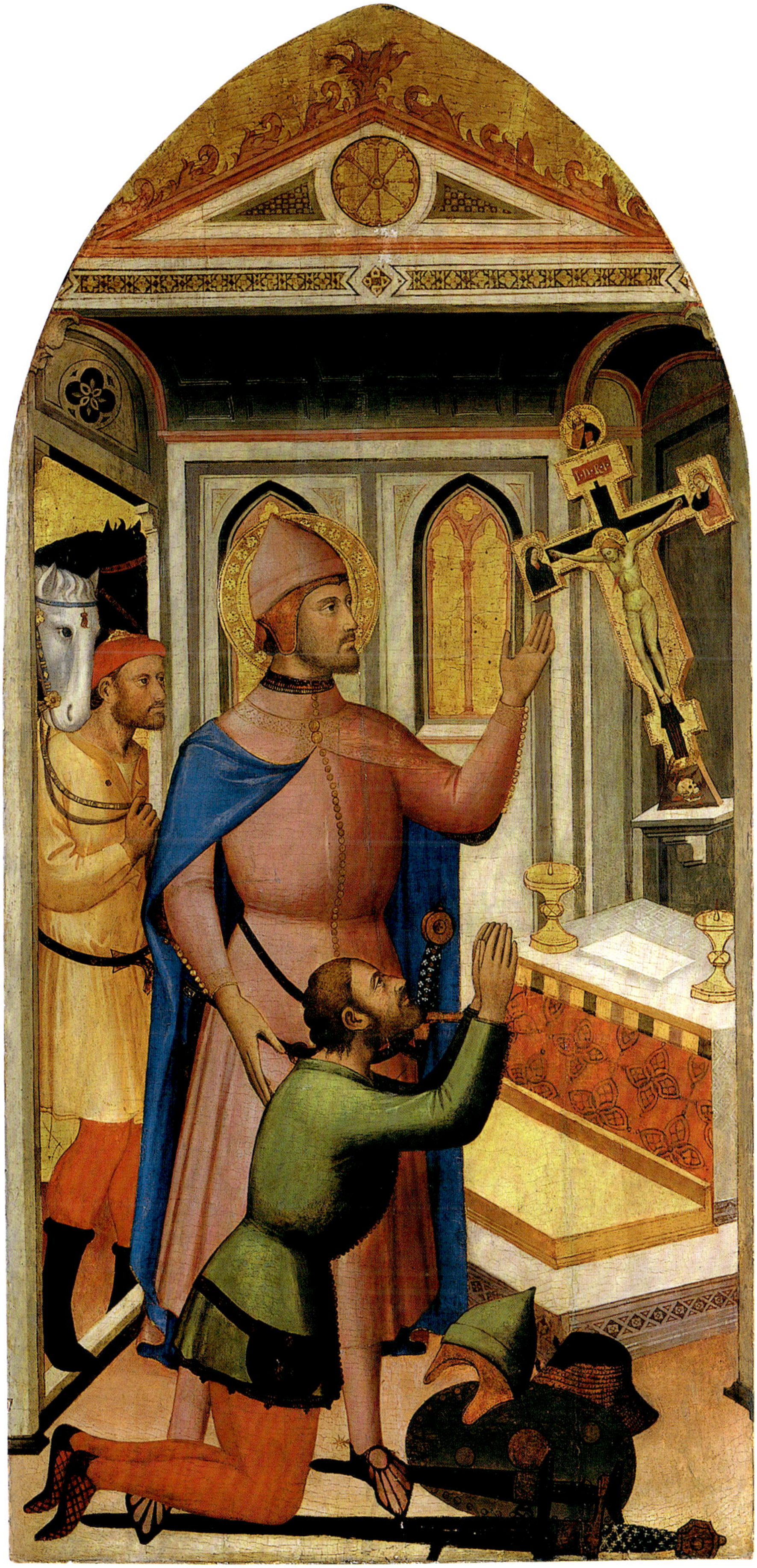

(opposite)
30. Leaf from an antiphonary with *Saint John Gualbert in an Initial S.* Umbria, early 16th century. Tempera, gold, and ink on parchment; 28 ¼ x 19 ⅞ in. (71.7 x 50.6 cm). The Metropolitan Museum of Art, Gift of Louis L. Lorillard, 1896, transferred from the Library (96.32.13)

(right)
31. Attributed to Niccolò di Pietro Gerini (active by 1368–died ca. 1415). *An Episode from the Life of Saint John Gualbert.* Florence. Tempera on wood, gold ground; 57 ¾ x 28 ½ in. (146.7 x 72.4 cm). The Metropolitan Museum of Art, Gwynne Andrews Fund, 1958 (58.135)

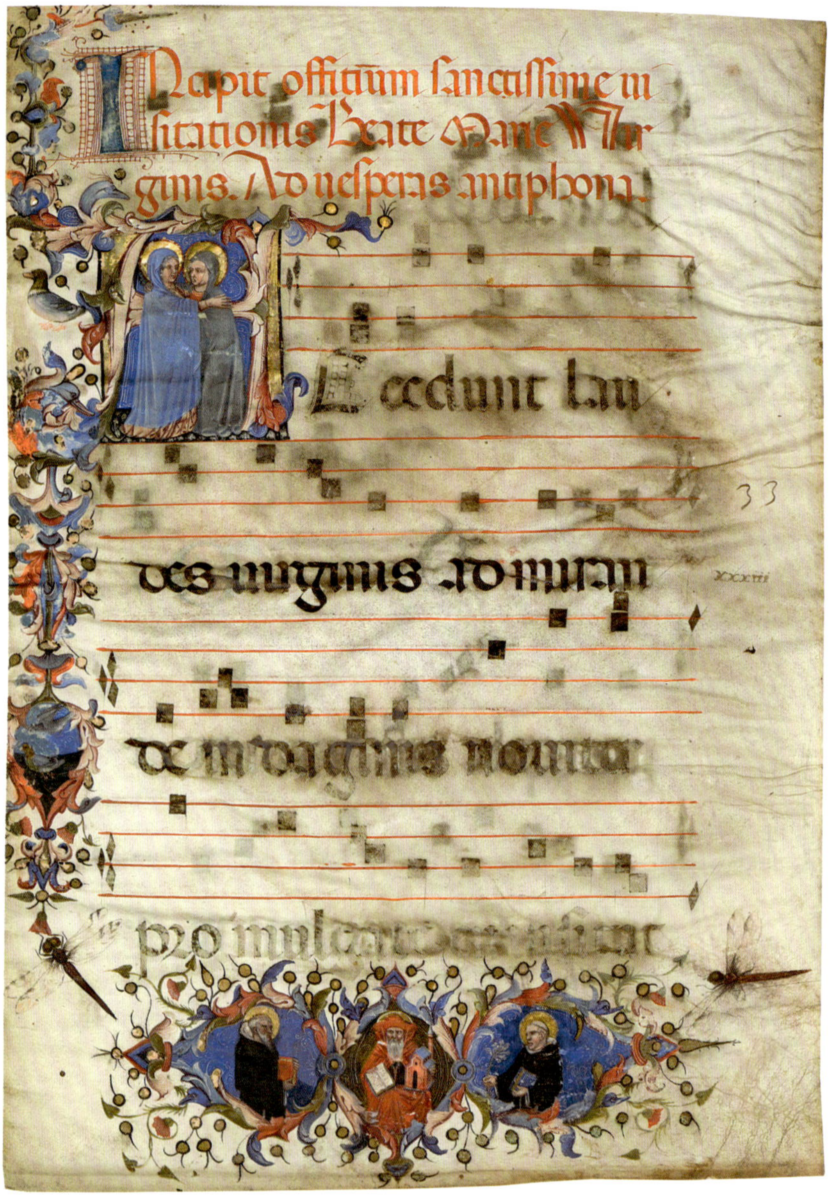

32. Leaf from an antiphonary with *The Visitation in an Initial A* and *Cardinal Adam Easton with a Dominican Saint and Saint Dominic*. Venice, ca. 1400. Tempera, gold, and ink on parchment; 19 ¼ x 13 ⅝ in. (49 x 34.5 cm). The Metropolitan Museum of Art, Bequest of Mrs. A. M. Minturn, 1890 (90.61.3)

that depicts the Visitation in an initial A at the top (figs. 32, 33). He wears the characteristic red vestments of a cardinal and holds a model of his parish church in Rome and an open book, presumably his newly written office. That the cardinal is flanked by Saint Dominic at the right and another Dominican saint at the left indicates that the antiphonary this page comes from was for Dominican use.

Monasteries benefited from patronage outside their immediate community. The archbishop of Lucca, Nicolò di Lazaro Guinigi, probably commissioned the choir books (see fig. 3) for the nearby Certosa di Farneta, one of 113 Carthusian houses dedicated to the Holy Spirit that were established in the fourteenth century. Born into a family of emerging great wealth that served as bankers to the pope in Rome from 1377 to 1392 and essentially ruled Lucca at the time, Nicolò rose meteorically from cleric to archbishop in a single year. The archbishop's arms appear on one of the sumptuously decorated miniatures in the Certosa di Farneta gradual, which are arguably more a reflection of his taste than the community's. The Carthusian order was known for its relative austerity: according to the rule of the order, for example, the church was to have no silver except the chalice for Mass, and services were to be held in darkness, except for a lamp for the choir book.

By decree Carthusian chants like the song in honor of Saint Stephen were to be sung in a plaintive manner: "As the duty of a good monk is rather to lament than to sing, we must so sing that lamentation, not the joy of singing, be in our hearts."[66]

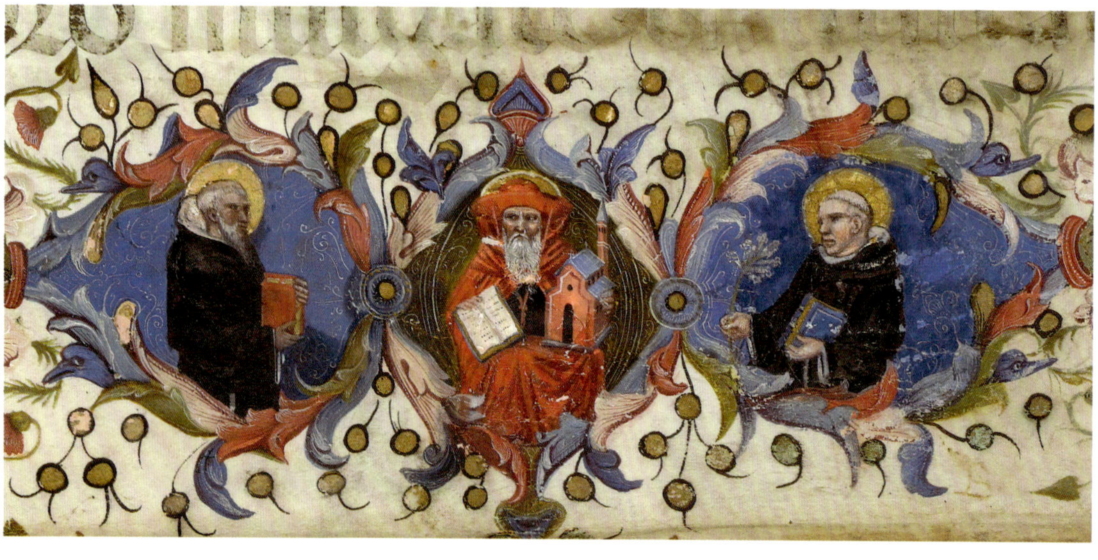

33. *Cardinal Adam Easton with a Dominican Saint and Saint Dominic* (detail of fig. 32)

One senses an official anxiety that the brothers, passing much of the day in solitude and subsisting on meager rations, might revel too much in the joy of singing together. In the more worldly atmosphere of Siena Cathedral, by contrast, officials enthusiastically sought eager singers, casting a wide net in their search and functioning much like modern-day scouts for professional athletes. One of their agents, reporting back from Genoa on June 20, 1447 (just as the artist Sano di Pietro [see fig. 66] was being paid for painting part of a psalter for the cathedral), announced that a certain Guglielmo Francioso, then at the cathedral in Genoa, was prepared to move to Siena and that he could be counted on to attract others from Florence. About another Genoese tenor he expressed some hesitation: "I think he sings well," he wrote, "but I don't know whether his voice is suitable for plainchant." And on a further cautionary note he added, "He's willing to come to Siena rather than to any other place. But I doubt that he's a stable person."[67]

In some instances the singers themselves served as the scribes, and even the illuminators, of manuscripts. In documents that have survived in Perugia from the early fourteenth century, Brother Andreas de Chatarno is described both as a cantor (choir leader) and as a good scribe, and Egidius de Scaltis is referred to as a "good cantor, most beautiful illuminator and scribe."[68] But this was certainly not the norm, and it does not account for the close "harmony" that often exists between word and image in medieval choir books.

### A is for *Ad te levavi*

### *An antiphonary for Sunday's daylight hours that begins "ad te levavi"*

The opening letter of a chant served as a recognizable heading, like a chapter number in a book. In choir books as in other types of medieval manuscripts, the first letter was often therefore enlarged and decorated to give it prominence.[69] On what appears to have been the first page of a volume of a thirteenth-century antiphonary (fig. 34), the letter P that begins the first response for the first nocturn of the Feast of the Ascension of Christ, "Post passionem suam" (After the suffering), is alive with twisting red and blue vines, and a doglike creature wraps itself around the upright of the letter, spewing red into its center.

When it was embellished with a figurative scene, the opening letter served as a memory key and ultimately as a focus of devotion for those who sang hymns of praise. Many subjects were standardized, but artists illustrating choir books responded in various ways, and at times with remarkable creativity, to the challenge of presenting their subject within the confines of a letter of the alphabet, whether a rounded C or O or a letter divided vertically like an M or horizontally like an E. A fictitious character in Reverend Dibdin's *Bibliographical Decameron* (1817) marvels at this and laments the loss of the practice: "I am quite charmed with such specimens; and wish in my heart that some Girolamo [dai Libri; see figs. 7, 10, 44] of the present day, would introduce the portraits of your Majesty and Privy Council, here solemnly assembled, within the graceful curvatures of a capital C or D."[70]

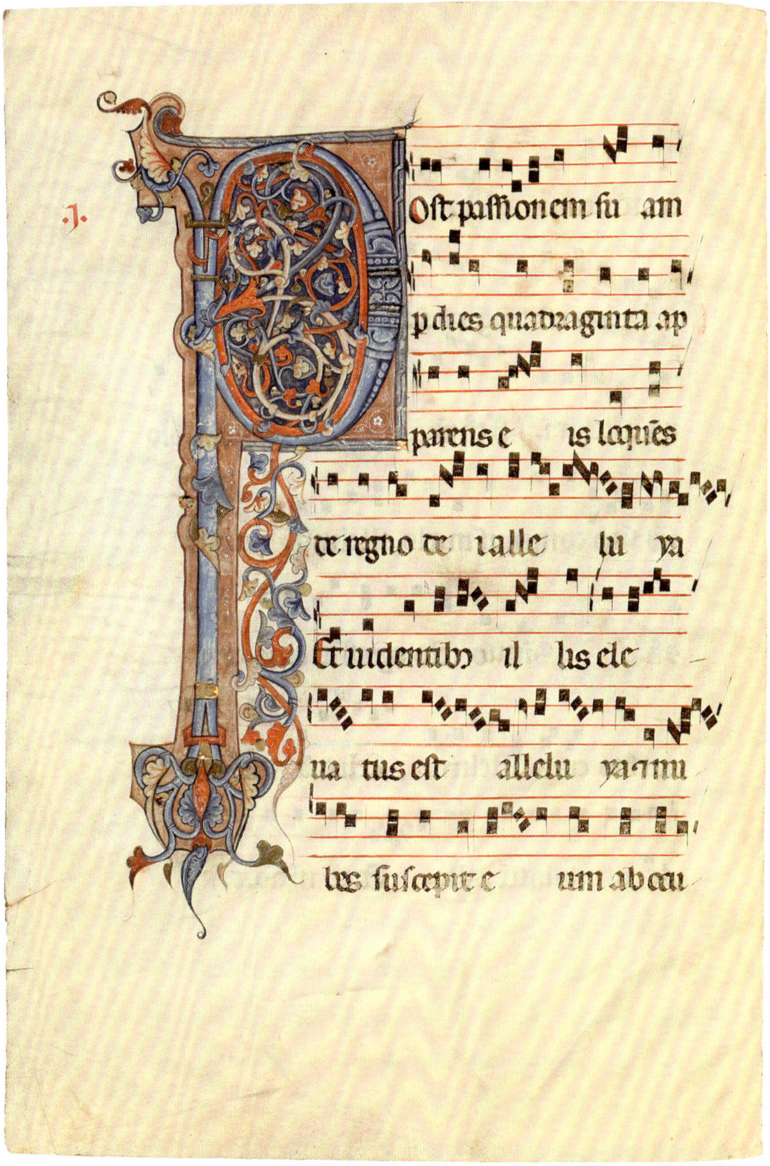

34. Leaf from an antiphonary with an initial P. Perhaps Arezzo, ca. 1250–60. Tempera, gold and silver leaf, and ink on parchment; 20 ½ x 14 ¼ in. (52 x 36.3 cm). The Metropolitan Museum of Art, Gift of Louis L. Lorillard, 1896, transferred from the Library (96.32.4)

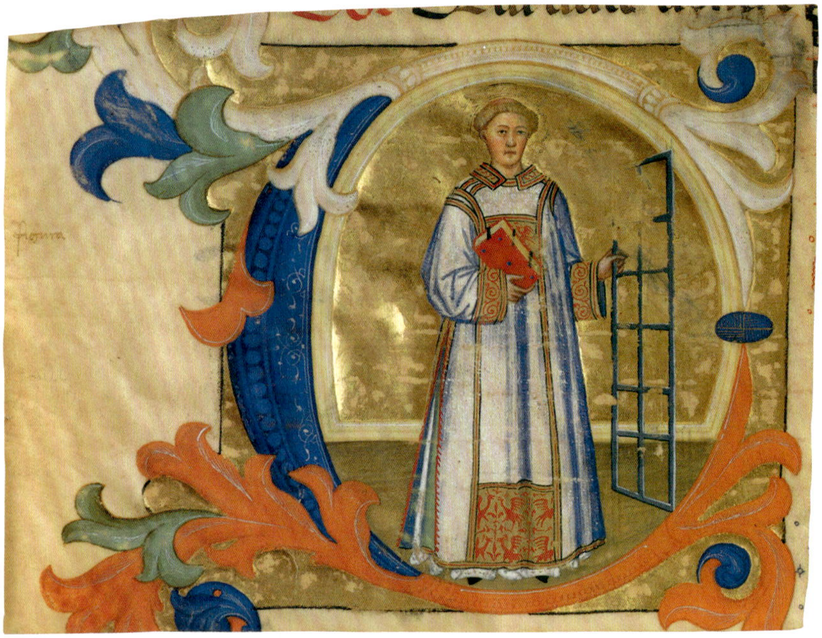


35. Don Simone Camaldolese (active 1375–98). *Initial C with Saint Lawrence*. Florence, ca. 1380–90. From a gradual. Tempera, gold, and ink on parchment; 5 7/8 x 7 1/2 in. (15 x 19.2 cm). The Metropolitan Museum of Art, Bequest of Mrs. A. M. Minturn, 1890 (90.61.2)

In a letter C for the Feast of Saint Lawrence on August 10 (fig. 35), Don Simone, who was born in Siena and worked in Florence in the late fourteenth century, conformed to the instruction penned in ink at the left that he should paint a *figura*. Accordingly, Lawrence, dressed as a deacon of the Church, stands in the oval of a completely closed letter C. In his right hand he holds a book and in his left what might appear to be a window frame but is in fact the grille on which he was martyred (a gruesome form of torture that has earned him widespread veneration as patron of the barbecue).

Depicting the standing figure of a saint holding an identifying attribute was one of the most common ways of illuminating a letter. The Master of the Brussels Initials (nicknamed for a manuscript he painted that is now in the Belgian Royal Library) followed the same general convention as Don Simone in presenting an image of Saint Stephen, who, like Lawrence, was a deacon (fig. 36). Stephen holds a book and a palm branch that signifies his martyrdom, and the two rocks and a brick balanced on the crown of his slightly bloodied head are reminders that the saint was killed by stoning.

The illustration of chants by very similar means often facilitates the identification of other cuttings apparently from the same manuscript. *The Initial S with Saint Stephen* and a cutting with a similar depiction of Christ Blessing in an initial E (fig. 37) provide a case in point. Snippets of text and music with a common stave height on the reverse of the two cuttings also argue for a shared origin. Though fragmented, the words on the reverse of the image of Christ Blessing determine unequivocally that it comes from an antiphonary for the season of Advent, and this is also a logical context for the Metropolitan's S. Chants for the Feast of Saint Stephen, celebrated on December 26, were traditionally bound with those for Advent and Christmas. A number of antiphons for Stephen's feast begin (as might be expected) with the letter S. On the Metropolitan's cutting the illuminator created a more compelling image of Saint Stephen by tucking the

36. Master of the Brussels Initials. *Initial S with Saint Stephen*. Bologna, ca. 1410–20. From an antiphonary. Tempera, gold, and ink on parchment; 5 1/8 x 5 in. (13.1 x 12.6 cm). The Metropolitan Museum of Art, Bequest of Gwynne M. Andrews, 1930 (31.134.1)

37. Master of the Brussels Initials. *Initial E with Christ Blessing*. Bologna, ca. 1410–20. From an antiphonary. Tempera, gold, and ink on parchment; 5 1/4 x 4 in. (13.4 x 10.1 cm). Private collection

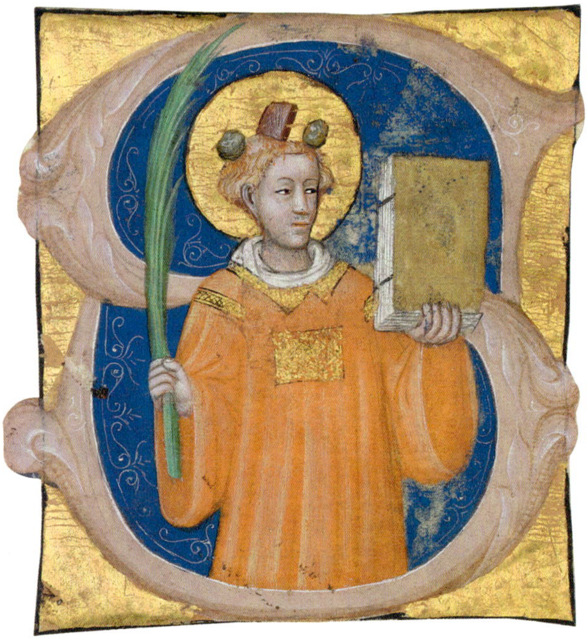

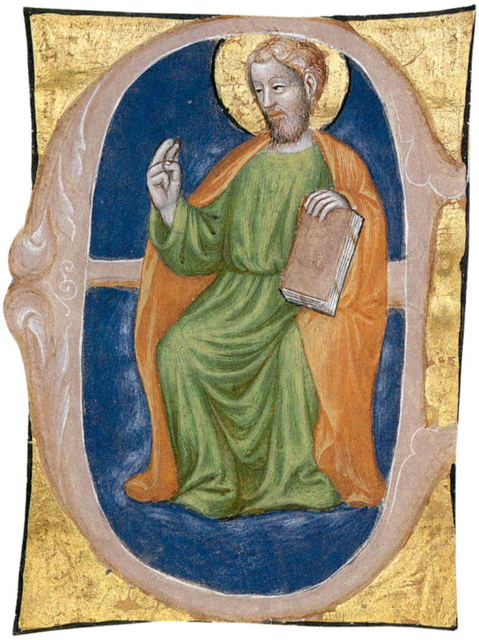

saint, hands coming forward and shoulders protruding slightly, behind and in front of the curves of the letter S so that it appears actually to exist in three-dimensional space.

Simple standing figures do not necessarily imply a simplistic treatment of a subject. The opening page of a Florentine antiphonary for Benedictine use (fig. 38), for example, presents two standing figures, each set under an arching loop of a letter M. The text, which begins "Missus est Gabriel Angelus ad Mariam virginem" (The Angel Gabriel was sent to Mary the Virgin), refers to the Annunciation, when the archangel announced to Mary that she would be the mother of Jesus. Especially when it is used to herald the Feast of the Annunciation (March 25; see also fig. 68), that text is frequently illustrated by images of Gabriel appearing to Mary. Here, however, at the beginning of Advent, the miniature is a sophisticated allusion to the link between the announcements of the births of Jesus and John the Baptist that is referred to in the gospels of both Luke and John. The bearded figure writing at the left is John the Evangelist, shown with his emblematic eagle. The older man is John the Baptist dressed as a prophet. The words on his scroll allude to the opening text of the gospel of Saint John, which refers to John the Baptist as *missus a Deo* (sent from God). Other leaves in the Museum's collection from the same antiphonary include illustrations of the celebration of the Mass (fig. 16), the Nativity (fig. 19), a miracle of Saint Benedict (fig. 53), and the first antiphon of Second Vespers for Christmas Day: "Tecum principium" (Yours is princely rule), showing God the Father wearing a tiara much like the pope's (fig. 39).

## Text and Image

***Let us sing with alert senses and a wakeful mind***

Even seemingly curious marginal details in choral manuscripts are sometimes explained by the text. In Zanobi Strozzi's B with David in prayer (fig. 9), for example, the angel grasping the stem of a leafy flower as he climbs determinedly onto the letter as if up a hill seems to refer to the metaphor in the text that compares the blessed man to a tree bringing forth fruit, whose "leaf shall not fall off" (Psalms 1:3).

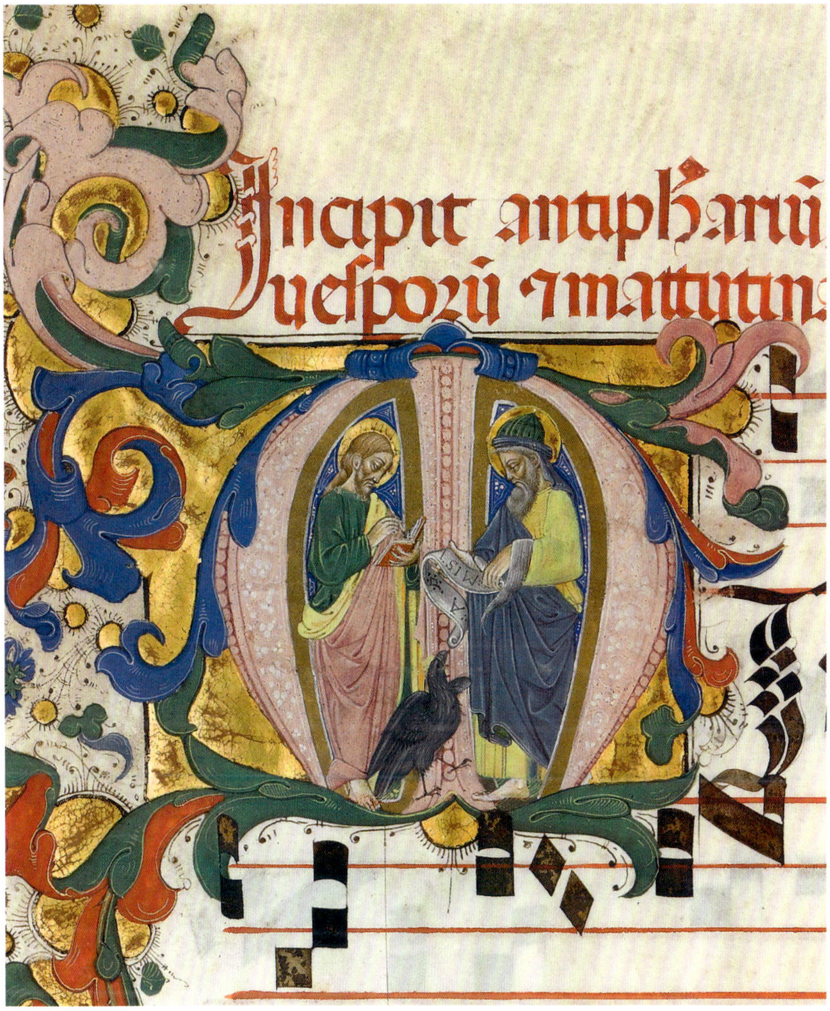

38. Master of the Riccardiana Lactantius. Leaf from a Benedictine antiphonary with *Saint John the Evangelist and Saint John the Baptist in an Initial M* (detail). Florence, second half of 15th century. Tempera, gold, and ink on parchment; leaf 22 3/8 x 15 5/8 in. (56.7 x 39.6 cm). The Metropolitan Museum of Art, Gift of Louis L. Lorillard, 1896, transferred from the Library (96.32.9)

In an illumination of the Assumption of the Virgin by Niccolò di ser Sozzo (fig. 40) there is a remarkable consonance between the image and the text (the first response for the first nocturn at the Feast of the Assumption, sung in darkness in the middle of the night): "I saw her fair as a dove taking flight over running waters." The Virgin Mary, in a diaphanous white gown, rises weightlessly and effortlessly toward heaven, her path gently guided by the chorus of nimbed and winged angels. Niccolò di ser Sozzo also painted large-scale commissions (his signature appears with that of Luca di Tommé on a polyptych in the Siena Pinacoteca), but he more frequently worked as a painter of manuscripts. In this he perhaps followed in the footsteps of his father, whose employment is known uniquely from documentation.[71] The subject of the Assumption recurs several times in Niccolò's work, not surprisingly given the importance of the feast in his hometown of Siena, whose cathedral is dedicated to the Assumption. (Already

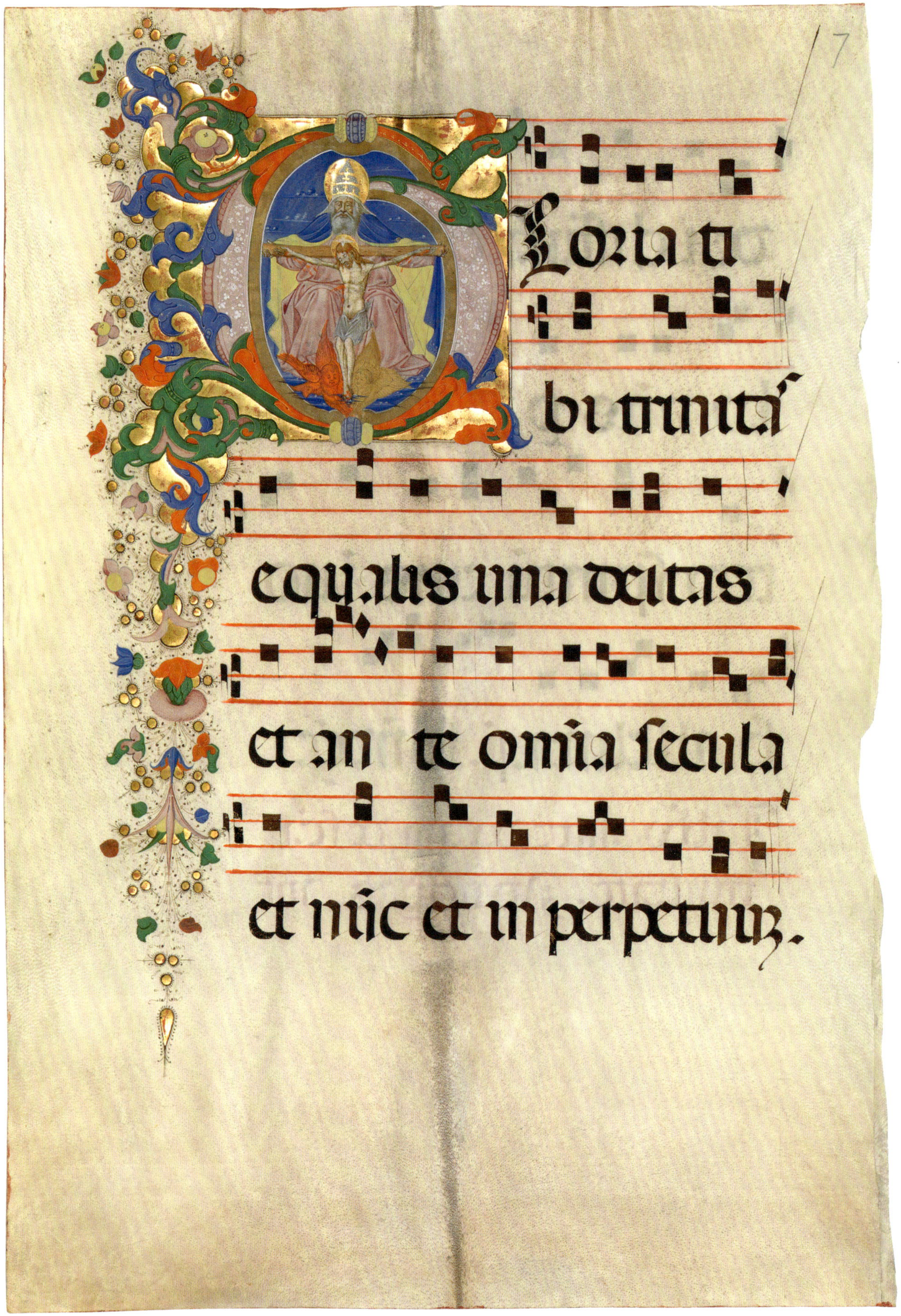
7
Loria ti
bi trinitas
equalis una deitas
et an te omia secula
et nuc et in perpetuu.

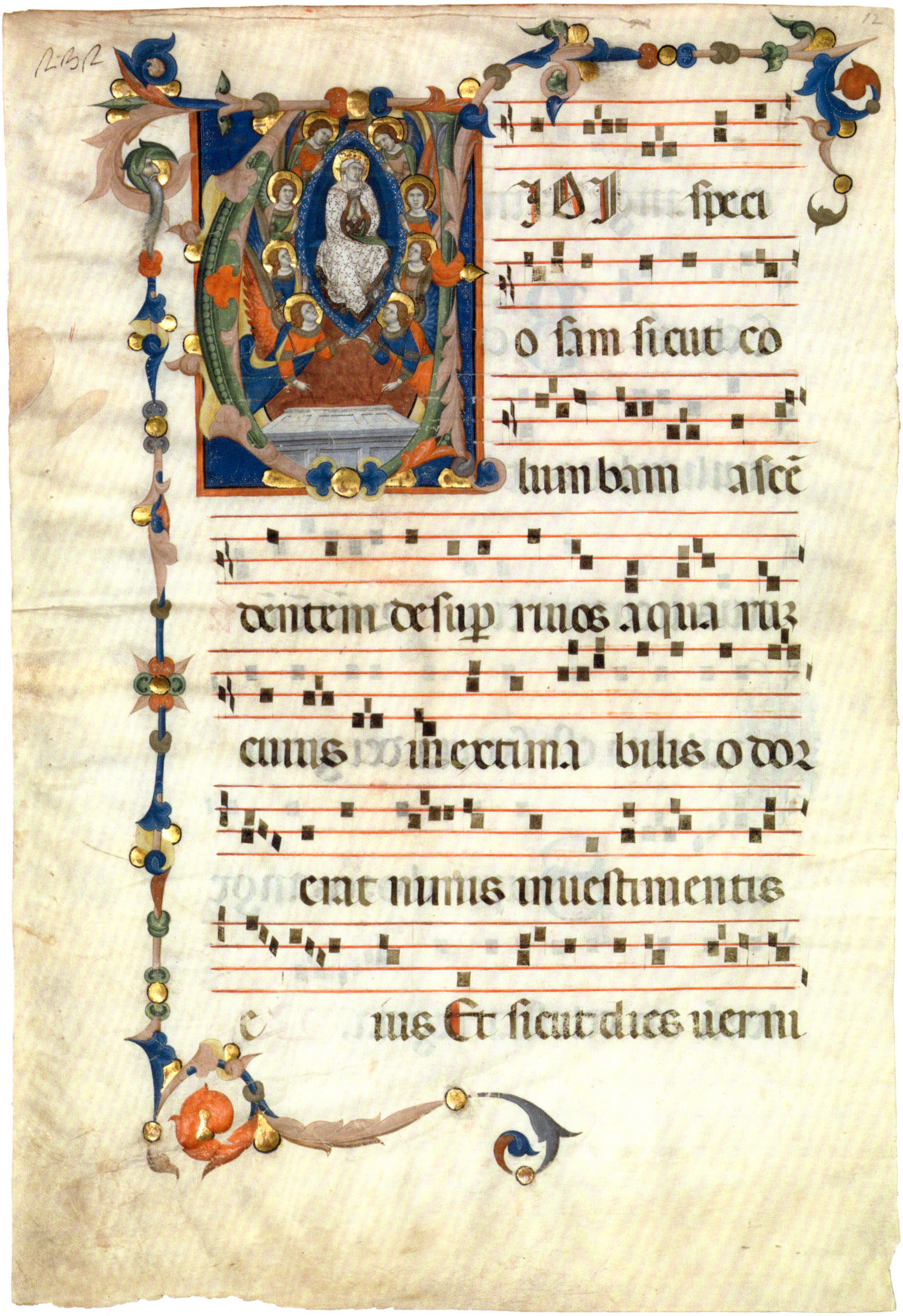

(opposite)
39. Master of the Riccardiana Lactantius. Leaf from a Benedictine antiphonary with *The Trinity in an Initial G.* Florence, second half of 15th century. Tempera, gold, and ink on parchment; 22 ⅜ x 15 ¾ in. (56.7 x 39.9 cm). The Metropolitan Museum of Art, Gift of Louis L. Lorillard, 1896, transferred from the Library (96.32.7)

(right)
40. Niccolò di ser Sozzo (active ca. 1334, died 1363). Leaf from an antiphonary with *The Assumption of the Virgin in an Initial V.* Siena, ca. 1340. Tempera, gold, and ink on parchment; 22 ⅝ x 15 ⅞ in. (57.5 x 40.4 cm). The Metropolitan Museum of Art, Gift of Louis L. Lorillard, 1896, transferred from the Library (96.32.12)

in the thirteenth century the celebrated Palio horse race had been established to coincide with the feast.) Niccolò signed his name on his representation of the same subject on the *Caleffo del'Assunto*, a public document of 1332–36 in the archives of Siena. And he also depicted the Assumption in a bound choir book for nearby San Gimignano and on a very similar isolated miniature of unknown provenance preserved in the Newark Museum in New Jersey.

The writings of a thirteenth-century canon of Siena Cathedral named Oderigo emphatically reinforce the visual evidence from these choir books of the importance of music at the Feast of the Assumption. Oderigo reported that the crowd attending services on August 15 was larger than at any other time during the year, and therefore the canons had to be prepared to give extra attention to singing the daily office.[72]

Sometimes the illuminations amplify and embellish the chant, so that what the monks saw was even richer than what they heard themselves sing. A letter S now in the Metropolitan (fig. 41), for example, illustrates a story recorded in chapter 12 of the Acts of the Apostles, in which Saint Peter is freed from prison by the intervention of an angel. The text of the hymn, partially preserved on the reverse of the cutting, echoes the angel's urgent instructions in the biblical text: "Rise, Peter, put on your vestment." The text then alludes to the chains falling from his hands, but the illumination traces the story beyond the text the choir was to sing—what is not spelled out is instead portrayed. The story starts in the compressed space in the lower part of the swirling letter S, where the angel leads Peter past two guards to the iron gate of the city. The miraculous opening of the gate is critical to the narrative, and the artist, apparently someone close to Pacino da Bonaguida (see fig. 57), has accordingly shown the iron bars cut open. The happy ending appears in the upper part of the S, where Peter is greeted at the home of Mary, mother of Saint Mark, by the faithful, including the servant woman Rhoda who first announced the escaped prisoner's arrival to a group of incredulous disciples.[73]

41. *Initial S with Saint Peter Liberated from Prison*. Florence, first half of 14th century. From an antiphonary. Tempera, gold, and ink on parchment; 6 x 4 ½ in. (15.1 x 11.5 cm). The Metropolitan Museum of Art, Gift of Bashford Dean, 1923 (23.21.3)

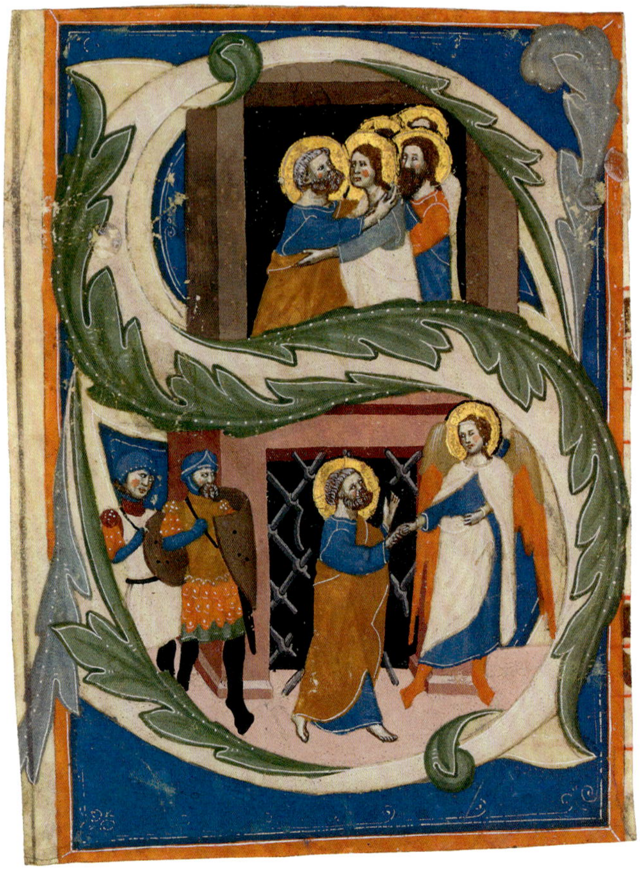

The text of the chant likewise provides key narrative details that inform the scene in a letter A by the Bolognese illuminator Nerius (fig. 42), who made dramatic use of the letter itself. The A cues the monks to sing an Easter antiphon: "An angel of the Lord came down from heaven and drawing near, rolled back the stone and sat upon it." Accordingly, a winged figure dressed in white (a "raiment as snow" according to the gospel text from which the antiphon is taken) perches on the edge of an open casket at the mouth of a cave hewn into a rocky crag. Three holy women intent on anointing the body of Jesus on Easter morning approach from the left, overcoming their timidity as they lean determinedly forward, their yearning sense of purpose contrasting sharply with the stillness of the cluster of armed guards who slumber at the right. (The gospel of Saint Matthew says that because of their fear of the angels, the guards "became as dead men.") Like the tomb itself, the top of the letter A is rolled open, as if by the electrical force of the angel with a face "as lightning" whose wings extend beyond the block of the illumination. Nerius used the natural division of the A to create two separate stage sets. A subsequent part of the Easter story is dramatically represented on the lower stage, where the same three women, recognizable by their brown, red, and gray-blue mantles, now approach from the right, prostrating themselves before the figure of Jesus, who has risen from the dead. The scenes conflate two gospel texts: that there are three women conforms to the gospel of Saint Mark (16:1–9), but their encounter with Jesus as they leave the tomb is in keeping with the gospel of Saint Matthew (28:1–10), from which the text of the antiphon is taken, though Matthew's account involves only two women: Mary Magdalene and "the other Mary."

By opening the top of the letter A, Nerius exposed the figures to the heavens. He did the same thing in another miniature cut from the same manuscript (fig. 43), but here the crossbar of the letter A separates the earthbound figures of a choir of singing monks from the realm of heaven, to which they nevertheless turn their gaze to behold a vision of God poised in the clouds and attended by angels. The monks' black habits, edged in white at the neck, suggest that the choir book from which both leaves came was for the use of a community of Augustinian monks, a mendicant order whose rule was adopted in 1256.[74]

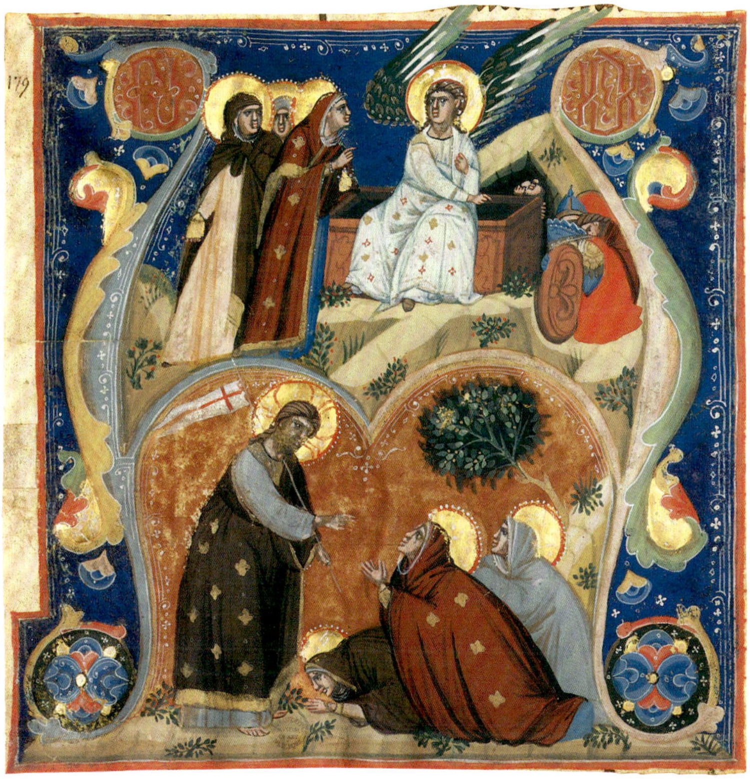

42. Nerius (active 1310–25). *Initial A with Scenes of Easter.* Bologna, ca. 1320. From an Augustinian antiphonary. Tempera, gold, and ink on parchment; 9 3/8 x 9 3/8 in. (23.9 x 23.8 cm). The Metropolitan Museum of Art, Rogers Fund, 1912 (12.56.1)

## The Letter as Stage Set

***How awesome is this place: . . . this is the gate of heaven***

The crossbar of the letter A has been expunged completely in an illustration attributed to Girolamo dai Libri (fig. 44). Letters on the reverse of the cutting confirm that the scene illustrates the same Easter antiphon as Nerius's miniature (fig. 42). The large blue mask, like an actor's, hanging from the left edge of the A heightens the sense that the drama is taking place on a stage. The crossbar of a letter A has likewise been eliminated entirely in an image of Saint Dominic holding up the church of Saint John Lateran (fig. 45). Indeed, the iridescent pink fishlike form curving up at the left barely hints at the letter. By emphatically squaring the letter off at the right, making it appear decidedly off kilter, the artist deliberately enhanced the image of the falling building, in which he has delicately drawn cracks descending from the structurally weak window openings. According to the story, which had appeared by 1246 in both Franciscan and Dominican legend, Pope Innocent III dreamed of Saint Dominic saving the church of Saint John Lateran from imminent collapse by supporting its walls with his own body. When he awoke, the pontiff took his dream as a sign that he should grant the saint's petition to establish the Dominican order. A few letters from incomplete words on the reverse, *ellectus* and *nduit* (fig. 46) belong in fact to the medieval introit used for the Common of Doctors of the Church and at the Feast of Saint

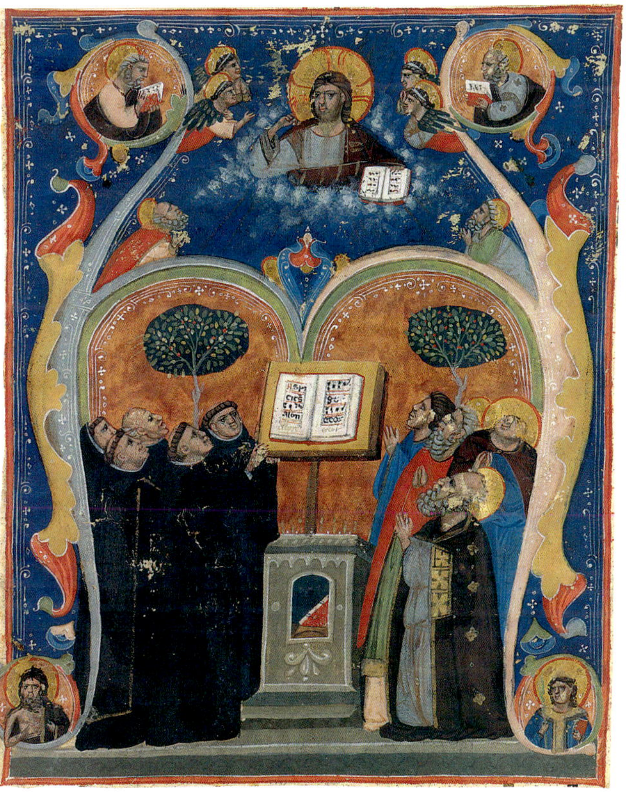

43. Nerius. *Initial A with Singing Monks and Saints.* Bologna, ca. 1320. From an Augustinian antiphonary. Tempera, gold, and ink on parchment; 9 1/2 x 7 7/8 in. (24.2 x 19.9 cm). Staatliche Graphische Sammlung, Munich (40096 z)

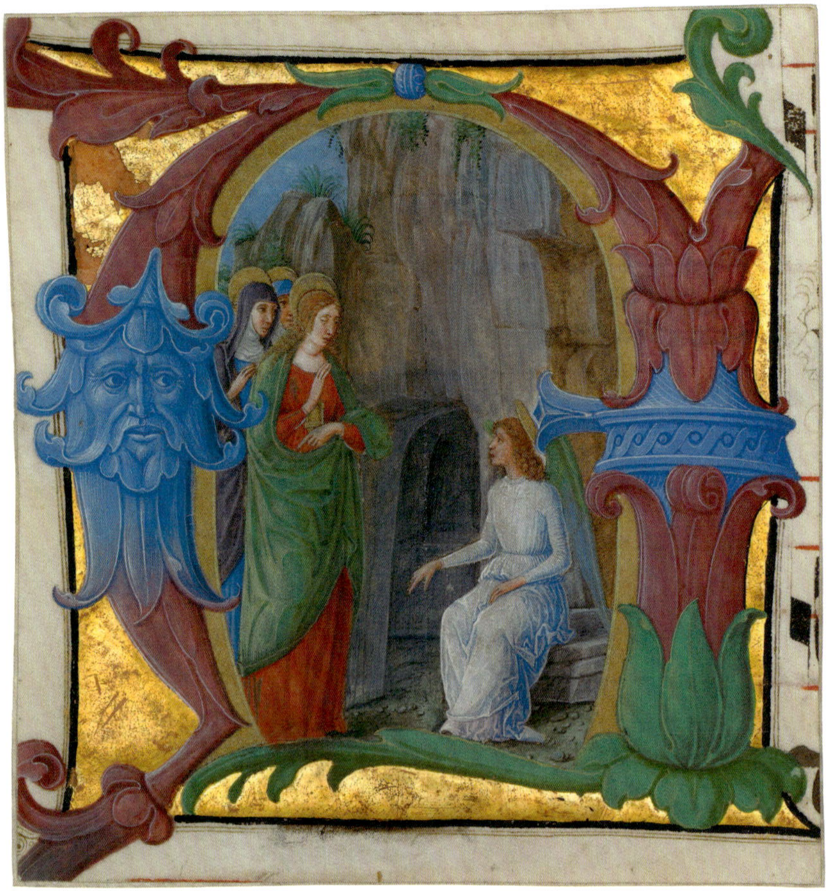

44. Girolamo dai Libri (1474/75–1555?). *Initial A with the Holy Women at the Tomb.* Verona, ca. 1490–1500. From an antiphonary. Tempera, gold, and ink on parchment; 9 x 6 ¼ in. (22.7 x 15.9 cm). The Metropolitan Museum of Art, Bequest of Millie Bruhl Frederick, 1962 (62.122.17)

Dominic: "In the midst of the church (*In medio ecclesiae*) he opened his mouth, and the Lord filled him with the spirit of wisdom and understanding (*intellectus*) and clothed him (*induit eum*) with the stole of glory." There must have been a large capital I on the original large parchment sheet, but then how to explain the A of the illumination? The historiated (i.e., with figures or narrative) letter A apparently heralded the specifically Dominican chant in honor of the order's founder, "Alleluia, O loving Father Dominic," that follows the introit. Thus in the gradual from which this illumination came, both the music and the images (I at the introit and A at the Alleluia) emphasized the importance of the feast of the founder of the order.

It is again as if as spectators at the theater that we witness the Birth of the Virgin set against the backdrop of a contemporary Florentine palace (fig. 47). Saint Anne's bedchamber, reminiscent of the interior of the Palazzo Davanzati, is richly appointed with cassoni and beautiful silks. Midwives and maidservants attend the new mother and bathe the infant. The artist, Don Silvestro dei Gherarducci, followed the composition of the same subject Pietro Lorenzetti painted for Siena Cathedral (fig. 48).[75] At the same time, he effectively used the arcs of the letter G to create a cozy, enclosed space. The curtain around Saint Anne's bed turns at the edge of the G (its reverse more orange in color) and begins to encircle it. We are afforded a peep at a more intimate world, protected by the letter. Stepping

45 and 46. Recto and verso of *Initial A with Saint Dominic Saving the Church of Saint John Lateran.* Lombardy, possibly Cremona, mid-15th century. From a Dominican gradual. Tempera, gold, and ink on parchment; 4 ¼ x 3 ⅝ in. (10.9 x 9.3 cm). The Metropolitan Museum of Art, Bequest of Gwynne M. Andrews, 1930 (31.134.5)

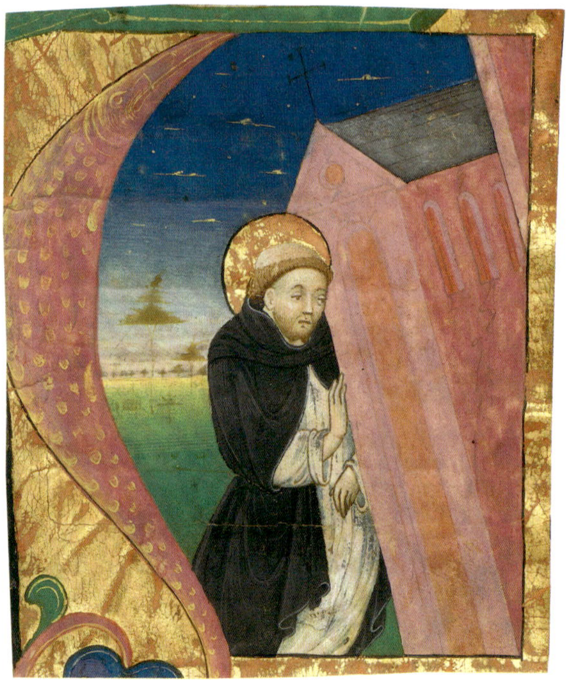

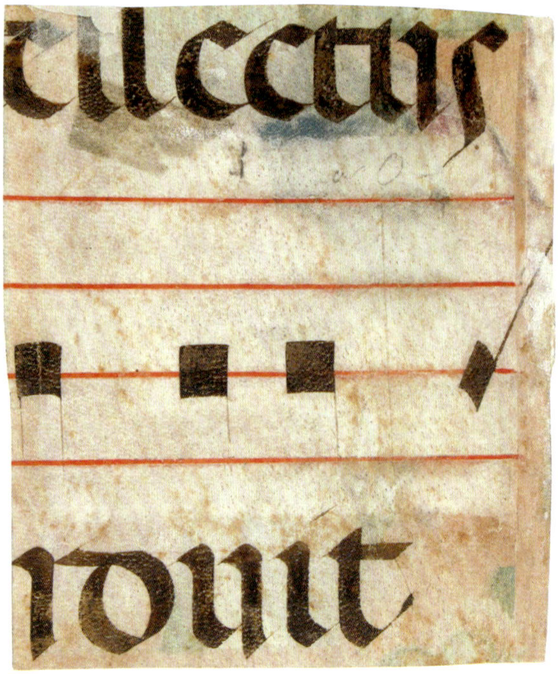

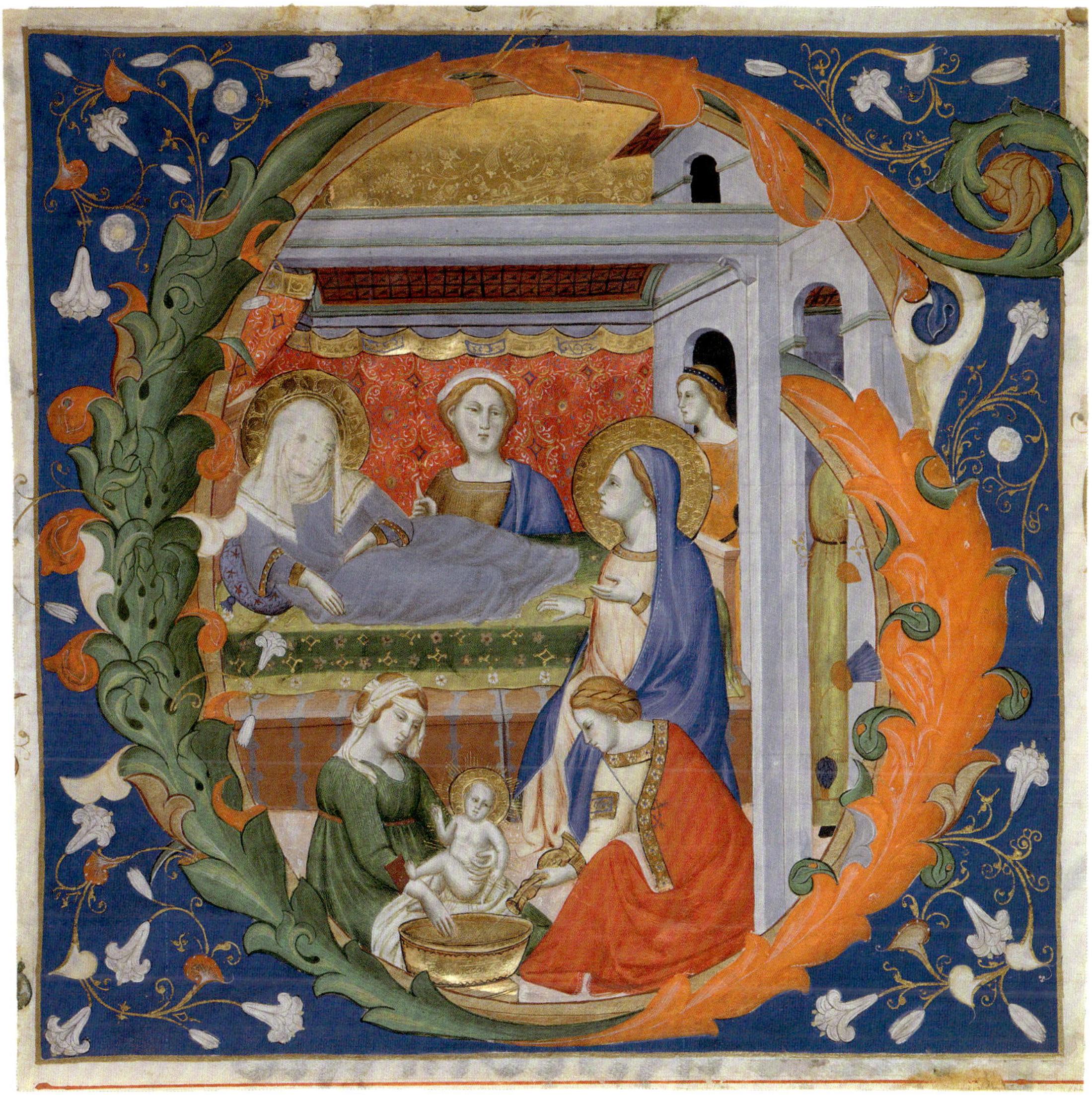

47. Don Silvestro dei Gherarducci (1339–1399). *Initial G with the Birth of the Virgin.* Florence, ca. 1375. From a gradual created for the Camaldolese monastery of Santa Maria degli Angeli, Florence. Tempera, gold, and ink on parchment; 11 ½ x 11 ¾ in. (29.2 x 29.8 cm). The Metropolitan Museum of Art, Rogers Fund, 1921 (21.168)

outside the letter is like stepping past the curtain at the edge of a stage, a point the artist has emphasized by completely obscuring the head of the maidservant who is about to exit the chamber at stage left.

To present the story of Joseph sold into slavery in Egypt by his brothers, the illuminator Giovanni Pietro da Cemmo embellished the familiar with the merest touch of the exotic (fig. 49). Young Joseph's brothers wear undershirts (*camice*) and stylish short tunics over hose known as *calze*. The torn knees of their red and blue hose suggest that they have fallen on hard times and are motivated as much by need as by jealousy of their brother's status as the favorite in the family. The Ishmaelites who buy Joseph are dressed as travelers in short tunics, tights, calf-high boots called *stivali*, and hats; one has a cape. The heads of a pair of unusual white animals, meant to be camels, offer the only hint at the location. The use of contemporary attire is of course a typical convention. It necessarily posits a connection between the biblical characters and late medieval society; in this case, it is clearly in keeping with the meaning of the story from Genesis (37:18–27) in a Christian context. During Lent, the Christian season of penitence preceding Easter, narrative subjects from Hebrew scriptures come into some prominence, as this period of fasting for forty days is considered to reflect Jesus' fast in the wilderness as well as the fasts of Moses (Exodus 34:28) and Elijah (I Kings 19:8). For medieval theologians, Lent was the season in which Christians should follow the example of the people of Israel.[76] Two other cuttings attributable to Giovanni Pietro da Cemmo preserved in Brescia similarly present episodes from the Hebrew scriptures. In scenes with Jacob and Esau (figs. 50, 51), the characters who have been on the road wear short tunics over hose and calf-high boots. In addition, the distinctive pastel palette, combining lilac and pale green, and the height of

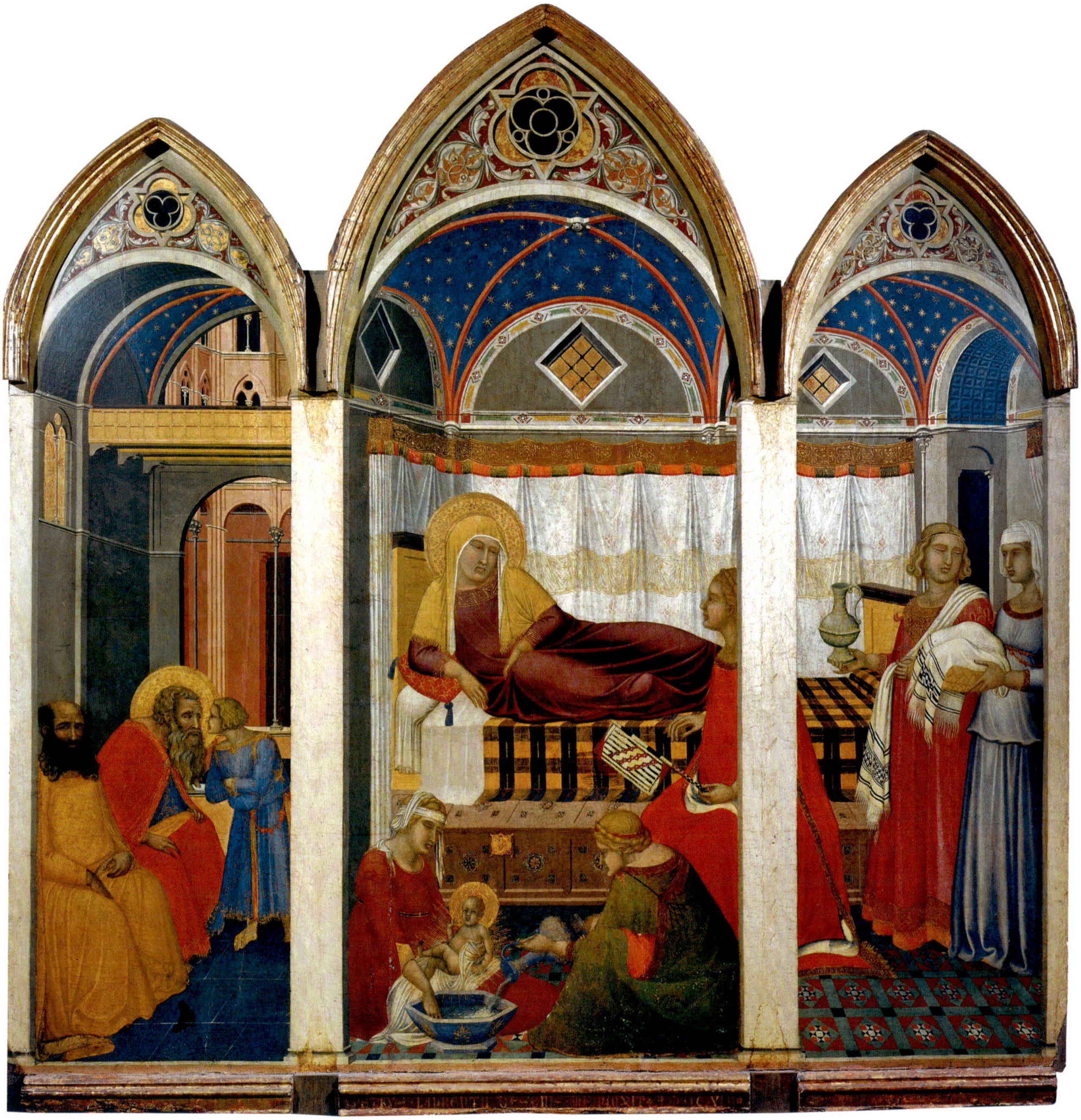

48. Pietro Lorenzetti (active ca. 1306–45). *The Birth of the Virgin*. Siena, 1342. Tempera and gold on panel, 6 ft. 2 in. x 5 ft. 11 ½ in. (1.87 x 1.82 m). Museo dell'Opera del Duomo, Siena

the staves on the reverse suggest that all three of these cuttings came from the same choir book volume for the season of Lent.

A sense of identification with events from Jewish history is even more explicit in an illumination of the Battle of the Maccabees (fig. 52). The Second Book of Maccabees recounts the revolt of the Jews following persecutions by Antiochus, king of the Hellenestic Seleucid empire in Asia Minor in the second century B.C.E. Under their leader, Judah Maccabee, the Jews ultimately achieved victory. They reestablished the Temple for Jewish worship in Jerusalem and achieved independence for the Jews in the land of Israel for about a century. This is the history celebrated by the Jewish holiday of Hanukkah. But medieval Christians regarded the Maccabees as prototypes of the Christian crusaders who fought to regain the holy city of Jerusalem from Muslims, whom they considered infidels.[77] Indeed, in the illumination, contained within a letter A with its crossbar removed, the Maccabees, under a red banner marked with a white M, appear as equestrian armored knights who advance across a stylized craggy landscape. The lollipop trees against a flat, star-strewn sky are standard in Bolognese illumination. Excised from an antiphonary, probably from a page for a Sunday during the long season after Pentecost, this miniature illustrates a response taken directly from the first chapter of the Second Book of Maccabees: "The Lord open your hearts in his law and commandments, and send you peace."

An antiphon of First Vespers on the Feast of Saint Benedict (fig. 53) appears at first glance to represent a miracle from Renaissance Italy. An artist called the Master of the Riccardiana Lactantius (after his illustrations of the writings of Lactantius, an early Christian philosopher, in a volume preserved in the Riccardiana Library in Florence) illustrated the story of Saint Benedict miraculously restoring a boy to life. The father who begged Benedict's help appears at the gate of the abbey in a brilliant blue fur-trimmed garment, bright red hose, a pink cape, and an ostentatious red cappuccio. His costume seems in keeping with an event that ended so joyously.

In the hands of the Florentine illuminator Mariano del Buono di Jacopo, two distinct scenes became vignettes of contemporary ceremony. The pomp of a papal procession embodies the introit of the Dedication of a Church (fig. 54), based on Genesis 28:17: "How awesome is this place: This is none other than the house of God; this is the gate of heaven." Set against the gray stone, the deep red, richly patterned velvet cope of the pontiff makes him the dramatic focus of the scene. The letter T serves as a barrier between the pope and the waiting church officials, the face of one obscured by the upright of the letter. A tonsured oblate peers out from the doorway, grasping its edge with his hand.

In another illumination even the inherently morbid subject of a funeral becomes an event full of

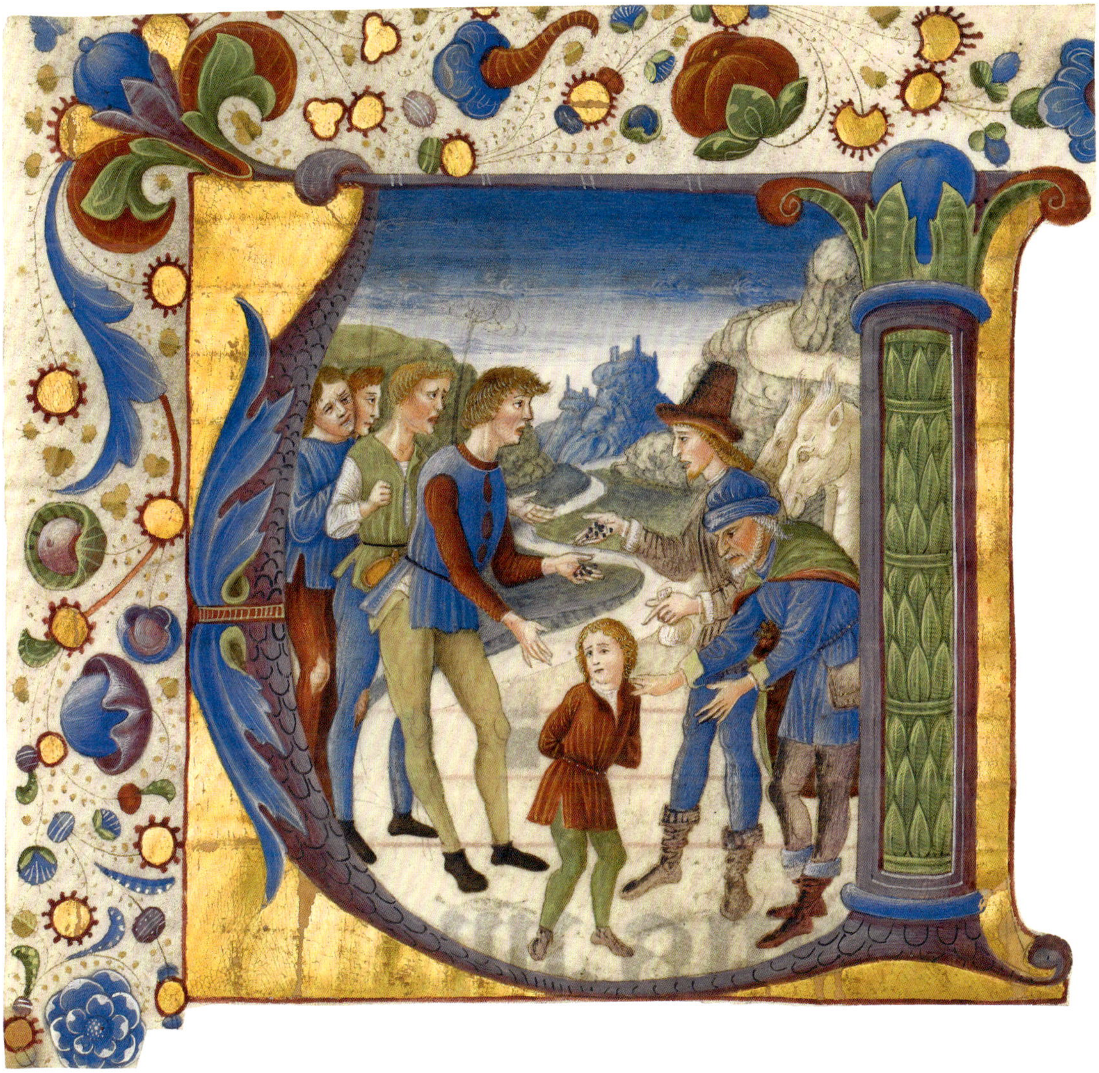

49. Giovanni Pietro da Cemmo (documented 1474–1507). *Initial V with Joseph Sold by His Brothers.* Brescia, ca. 1490. From an antiphonary, perhaps created for the Augustinian monastery of San Barnaba, Brescia. Tempera, gold, and ink on parchment; 6 ¾ x 7 in. (17.1 x 17.9 cm). The Metropolitan Museum of Art, Gift of Coudert Brothers, 1888 (88.3.50)

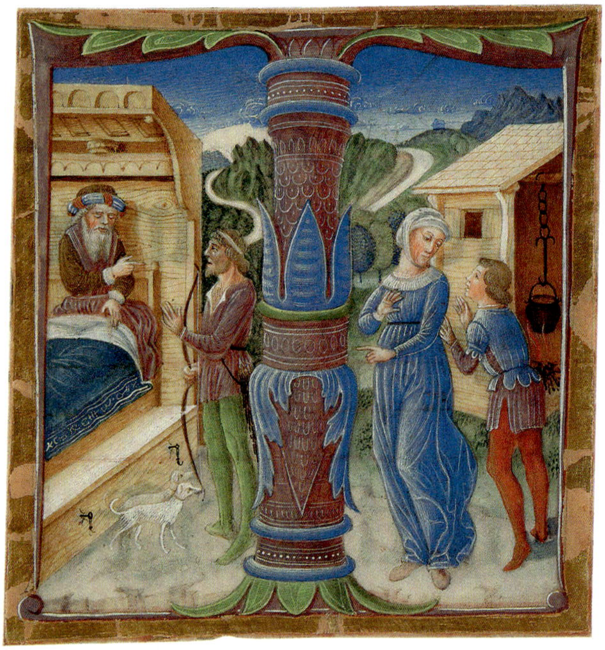

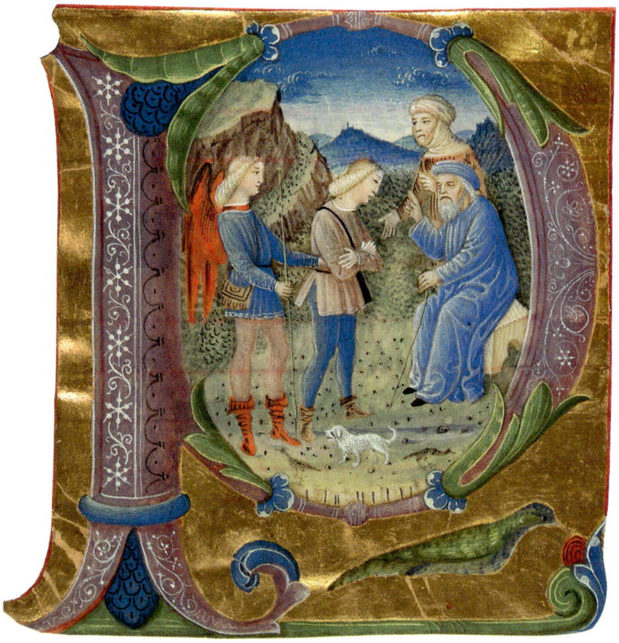

50 and 51. Giovanni Pietro da Cemmo. *Initial I with Esau Departing for the Hunt* (left) and *Initial P with the Benediction of Jacob* (right). Brescia, ca. 1490. From an antiphonary, perhaps created for the Augustinian monastery of San Barnaba, Brescia. Tempera, gold, and ink on parchment; each 5½ x 5½ in. (14 x 14 cm). Pinacoteca Tosio Martinengo, Brescia (inv. 52, 42)

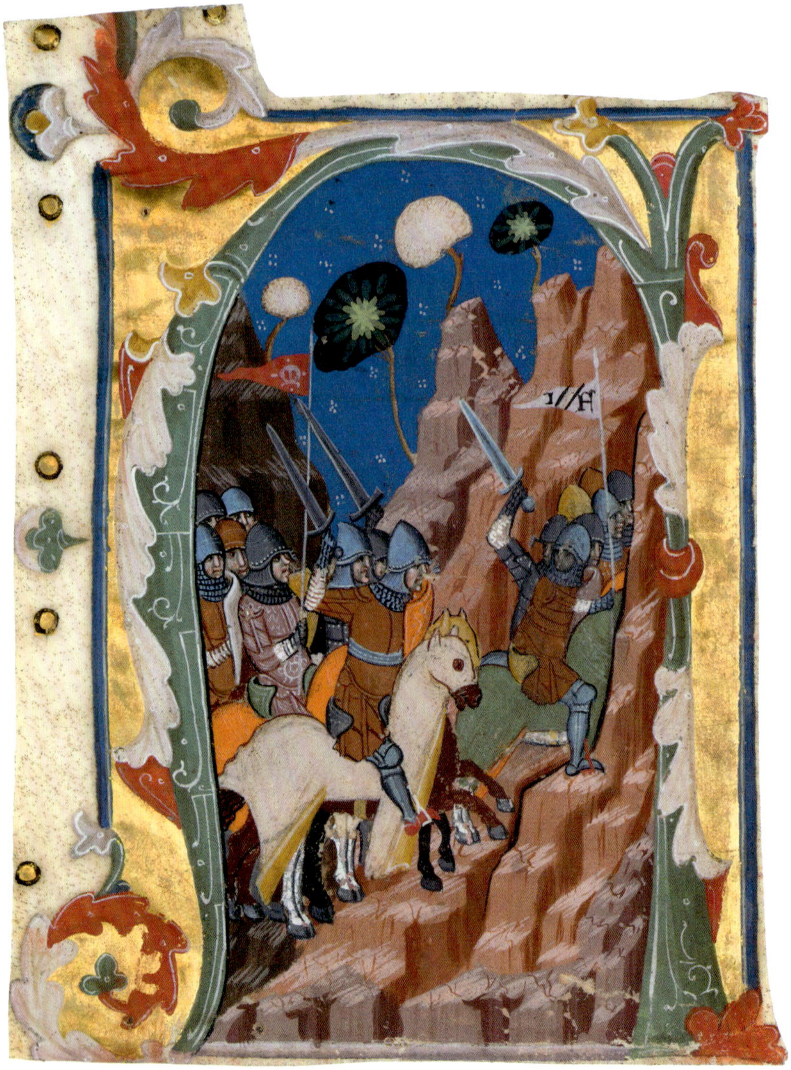

life as an array of mourners, some in pink robes, some with orange hose, and some in fur-trimmed tunics, process to a church (fig. 55). In this portrayal of a funeral procession Mariano del Buono surpassed even his own painting of the pope arriving at a church. The deceased gentleman, laid out on a flat bier as Florentine law permitted,[78] with a patterned pink silk pall and a matching pillow with blue tassels, is only partially visible, his lower torso obscured by the letter R of "Requiem." Only the feet of some of the pallbearers are visible as the mourners wind their way across the shallow proscenium beneath the letter. The artist depended on his audience to imagine as well that offstage, somewhere outside the picture plane, the entire procession turns, winding its way back into the field of the

52. *Initial A with the Battle of the Maccabees.* Probably Bologna, ca. 1360–70. From an antiphonary. Tempera, gold, and ink on parchment; 8 x 6 in. (20.4 x 15.1 cm). The Metropolitan Museum of Art, Gift of Bashford Dean, 1923 (23.21.4)

53. Master of the Riccardiana Lactantius. Leaf from a Benedictine antiphonary with *Saint Benedict Resuscitating a Boy in an Initial D.* Florence, second half of 15th century. Tempera, gold, and ink on parchment; 21 ⅞ x 15 ⅞ in. (55.5 x 40.4 cm). The Metropolitan Museum of Art, Gift of Louis L. Lorillard, 1896, transferred from the Library (96.32.11)

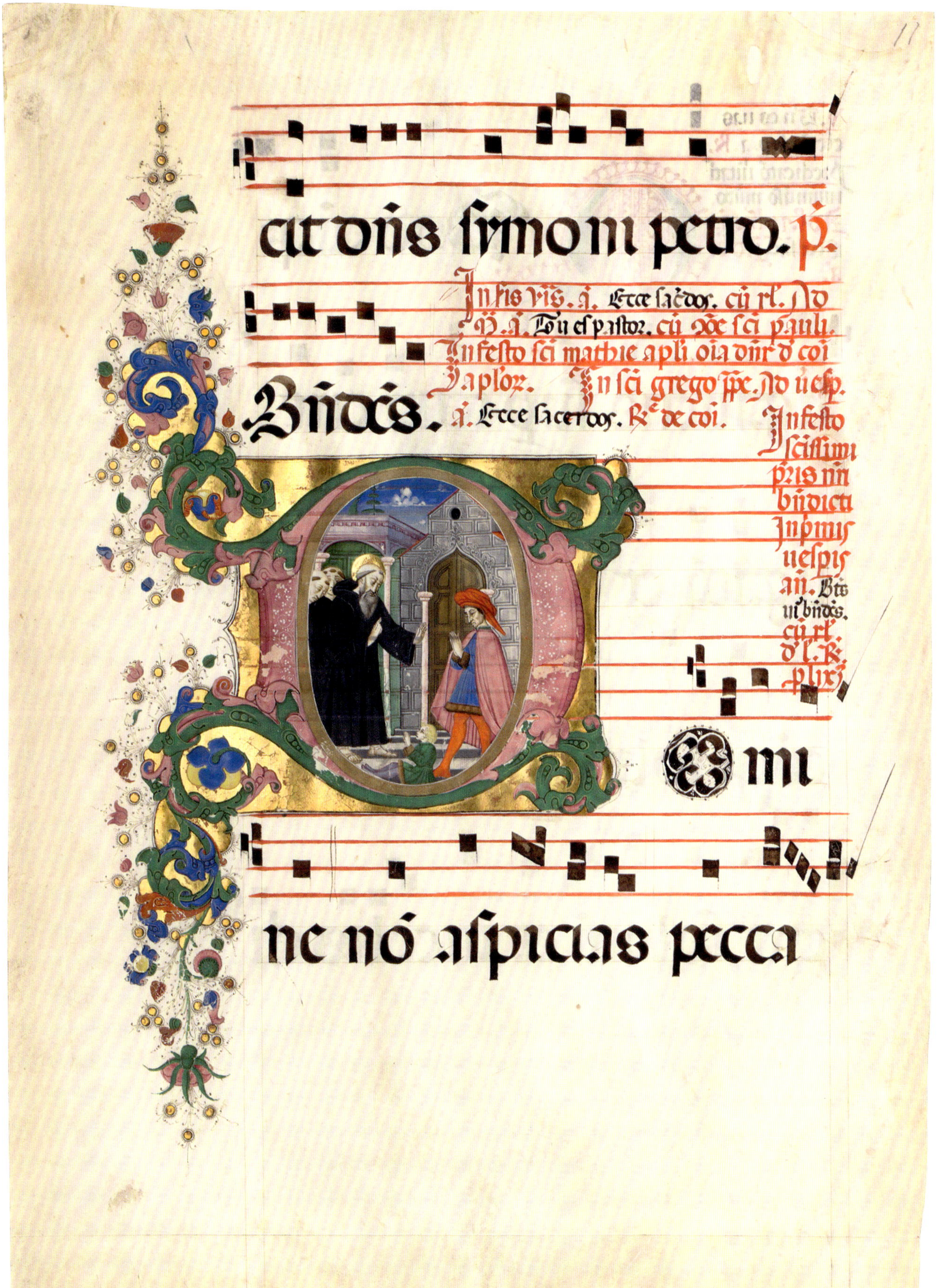

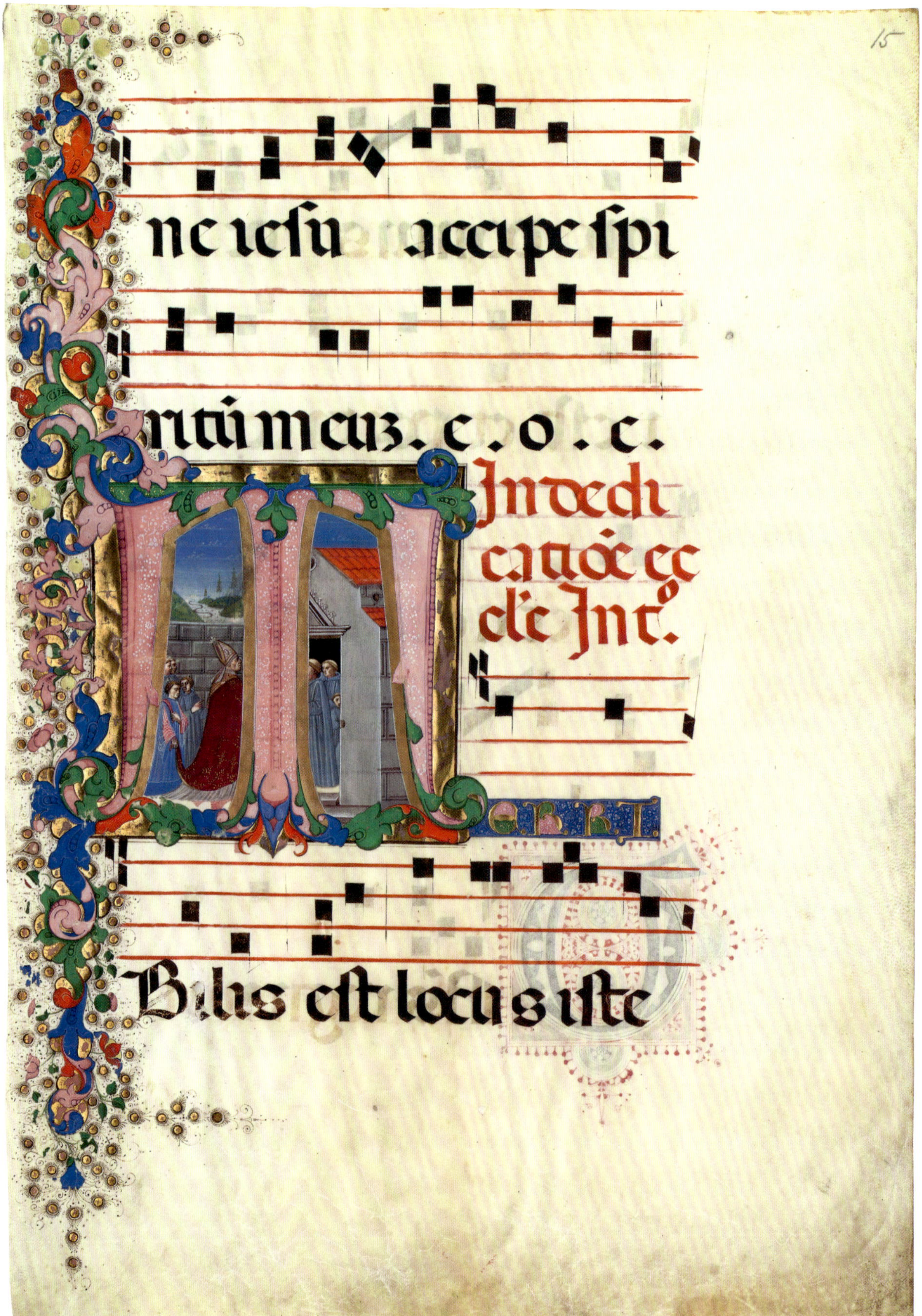


54. Mariano del Buono (1433–1504). Leaf from a gradual with *The Dedication of a Church in an Initial T.* Florence, second half of 15th century. Tempera, gold, and ink on parchment. 28 ¼ x 20 in. (71.6 x 50.8 cm). The Metropolitan Museum of Art, Gift of Louis L. Lorillard, 1896, transferred from the Library (96.32.15)

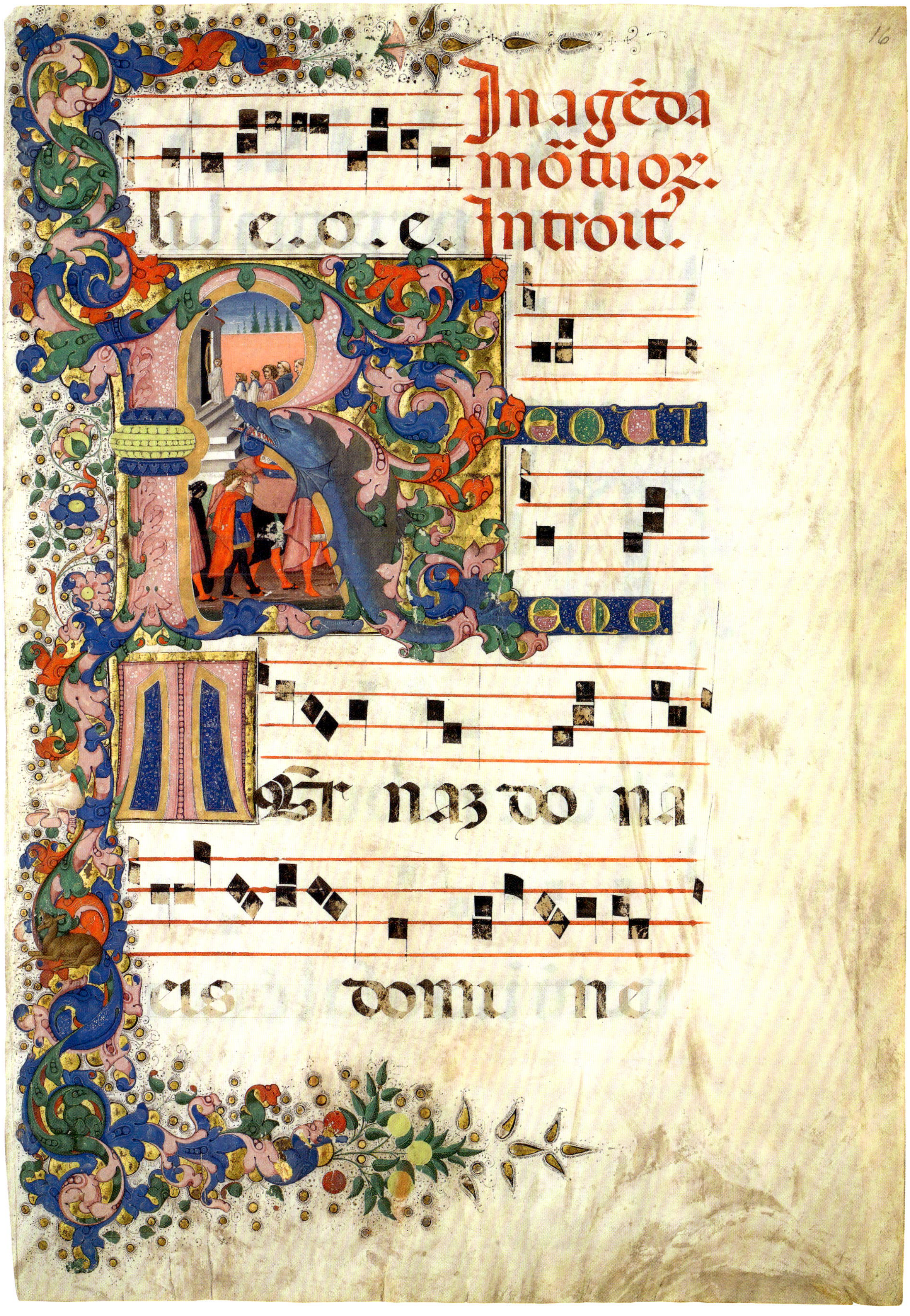


55. Mariano del Buono. Leaf from a gradual with *A Funeral Procession in an Initial R*. Florence, second half of 15th century. Tempera, gold, and ink on parchment; 28 1/8 x 20 1/8 in. (71.5 x 51 cm). The Metropolitan Museum of Art, Gift of Louis L. Lorillard, 1896, transferred from the Library (96.32.16)

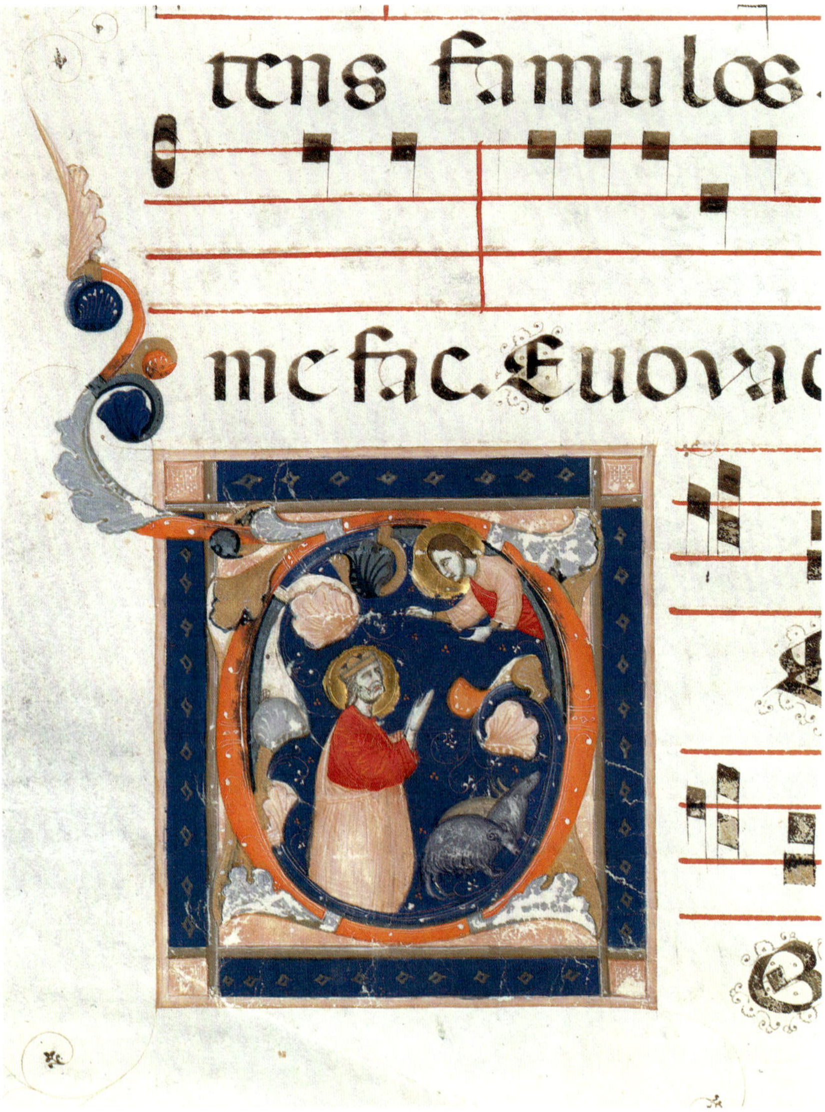

56. Fulget Master. Leaf from an antiphonary with *King David in an Initial D* (detail). Rimini, before 1310. Tempera, gold, silver, and ink on parchment; leaf 21 ¾ x 15 ¼ in. (55.3 x 38.7 cm). Anonymous loan

57. Pacino di Bonaguida (active 1303–ca. 1340). *The Martyrdom of Saint Bartholomew*. Florence, ca. 1340. From the laudario created for Sant'Agnese, Florence. Tempera, gold, and ink on parchment; 18 ½ x 13 ¾ in. (47 x 35 cm). The Metropolitan Museum of Art, The Cloisters Collection, 2006 (2006.250)

letter to climb the stairs into the church. Mariano del Buono presented but a glimpse of a narrative scene set in a naturalistic landscape juxtaposed with a framing initial covered with highly inventive ornament. Whereas the upright of the letter R is delicately painted with tiny white flowers on a soft pink ground that are similar to the decoration in the smaller letters of the word "Requiem," the descender has turned into a dragonlike creature with a monstrous snout and jaws that seem to threaten the safety of the faithful. Are these the jaws of death or the mouth of Hell that is commonly found in medieval imagery? Are the anxious crucifer and the youth in pink who turn to glance in our direction simply looking at the body of the deceased, or do they somehow perceive the threat to their own vitality the dragon represents?

Another ferocious dragon frames the scene of the Assumption of the Virgin linked to the Ferrarese artist Cosmè Tura (see fig. 26). The start of the text of the antiphon translates as: "Mary hath been taken up into heaven, the angels rejoice, and blessing God, praise him." The miraculous subject is presented in a rather conventional way, with the kneeling apostles gazing heavenward. What makes the miniature truly astounding is the muscular, virile green dragon whose body and wings simultaneously form the letter A and separate earth and heaven.

Only rarely was the standard formula of presenting a scene within the frame of a letter abandoned. At first glance this appears to be the case in an image of King David as a shepherd by an artist in the circle of the prolific master Neri da Rimini known as the Fulget Master (fig. 56). In fact, however, the letter D is contained within and partly disguised by a square frame. The ascender of the letter pushes out of the enclosing square with the vitality of an ivy vine. Faint notations in Latin in the margin, which were intended to be erased when the page was finished but were somehow overlooked, specify the illustration: "King kneeling with herd of sheep and Jesus[?] above." The curve of the letter provides the confines for the little herd's antics.

On a leaf with the martyrdom of Saint Bartholomew (fig. 57) the introductory framing letter has disappeared altogether. Perhaps the artist, Pacino di Bonaguida, departed from monastic convention in this manuscript because it represented a new kind of hymnal. Known as a laudario, it was intended for the use of *laudesi*, citizens' groups that gathered for spiritual support, prayer, and the singing of the *laude*, or sacred songs. These confraternities echoed centuries-old monastic practice, but they sang in Italian rather than Latin. Mendicant preachers encouraged the growth of such lay societies. Florence had twenty by the end of the thirteenth century; forty existed in Perugia in the fourteenth.[79] Like modern-day university fraternities or the society of Masons, *laudesi* subjected their members to codes of secrecy, induction rites, and conventions of dress. The participation of women, a number of whom are represented in the margins of other pages of this same laudario, increased during the fourteenth and fifteenth centuries.[80]

The Metropolitan's arresting image of Saint Bartholomew comes from the most important manuscript created in Florence in the first half of the fourteenth century: a laudario commissioned by the confraternity of Saint Agnes for use at the

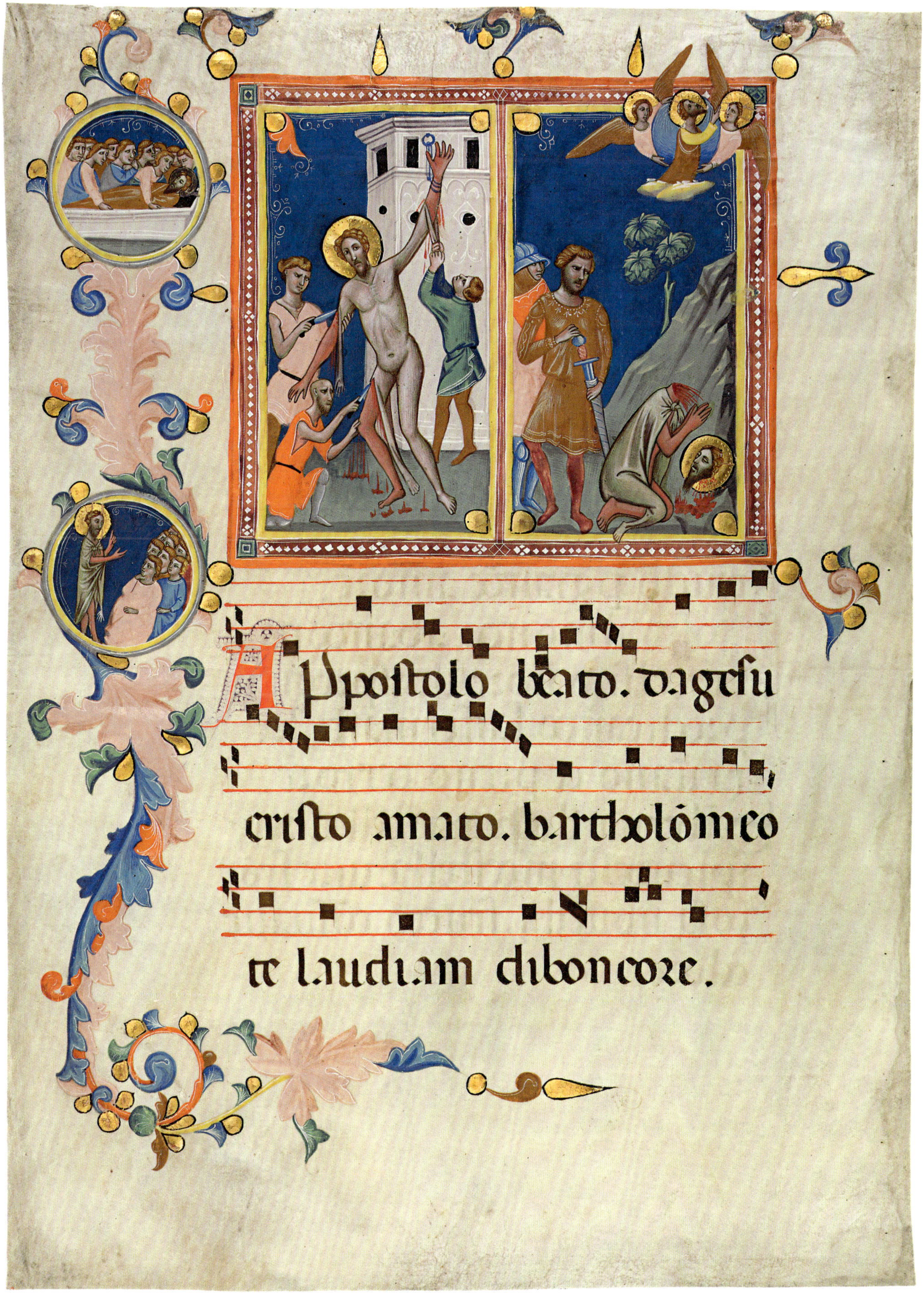
Appostolo beato. dagesu
cristo amato. bartholomeo
te laudiam dibon core.

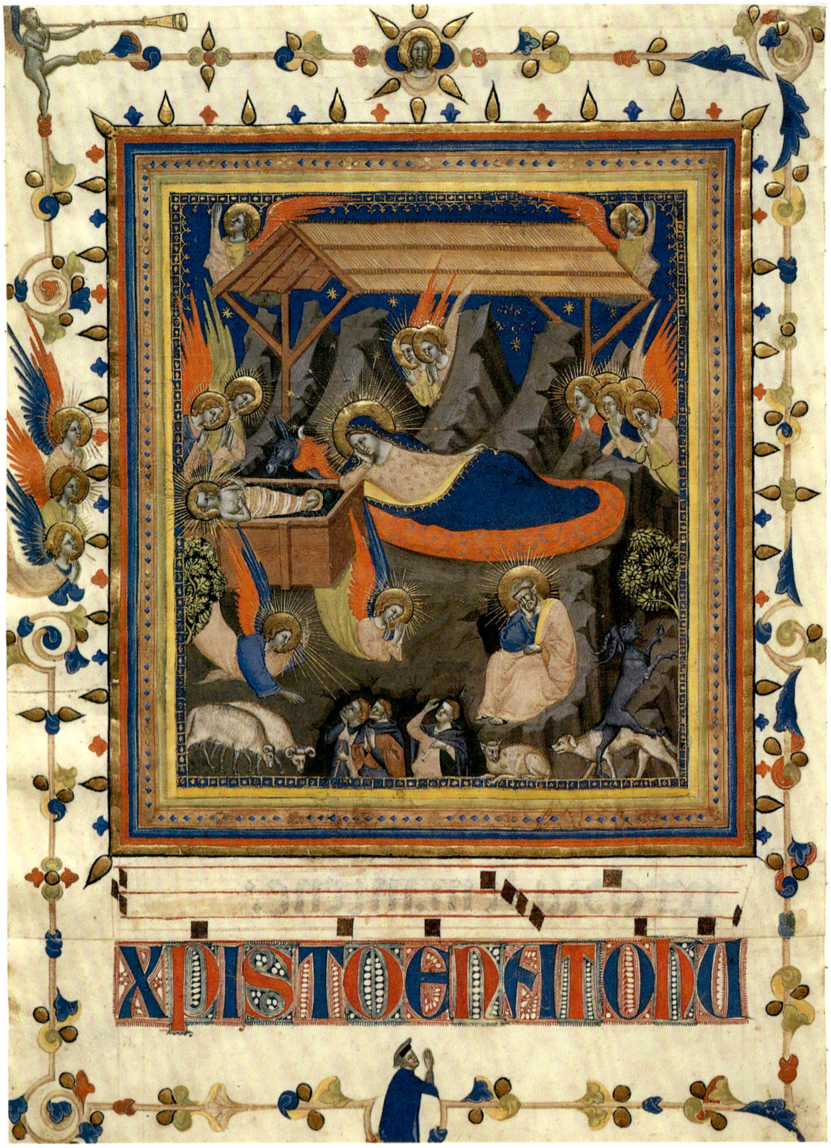

58. Master of the Dominican Effigies (active 1328–50). *The Nativity and the Annunciation to the Shepherds.* Florence, ca. 1340. From the laudario created for Sant'Agnese, Florence. Tempera, gold, and ink on parchment; 14 3/8 x 10 5/8 in. (36.5 x 27.1 cm). National Gallery of Art, Washington, D.C., Rosenwald Collection (1949.5.87, B-15393)

church of Santa Maria del Carmine. Pacino di Bonaguida painted *The Martyrdom of Saint Bartholomew* as if it were a small diptych. At the left, Bartholomew is chained to a city gate and flayed. His graceful pose transforms the horror of his martyrdom into a scene of dancelike grace. In a stop-action scene at the right, the saint has just been beheaded; his headless body still kneels in prayer, and his own skin is tied around his neck as a mantle. At the upper right angels accompany Bartholomew's tiny soul to heaven. In the lowermost roundel at the left, he is shown preaching to a crowd in India, where he was believed to have spread the gospel. In the roundel above, his body is being laid in his tomb.

## Illuminators of Choir Books

***They deserved the applause not only of monarchs, but even of professors in the best age of art***

What we know of the careers of Pacino di Bonaguida and other medieval artists responsible for the illuminations in the Metropolitan's collection offers interesting insights into the creation of choir books. Pacino, for instance, is mentioned as a painter in documents dating to 1303. Between 1327 and 1330 his name appears among the members of the Florentine painters' guild, which was linked to the guild of physicians and apothecaries.[81] His only signed work is a monumental painting of the Crucifixion preserved in the Accademia in Florence that bears a partly legible date, probably 1340.[82] The *Crucifixion* appears to be contemporary with the laudario he painted for Santa Maria del Carmine; the fact that the laudario was completed by another artist, dubbed the Master of the Dominican Effigies, may suggest either deliberate collaboration or that the laudario was incomplete at the time of Pacino's death. Those pages illuminated by the Master of the Dominican Effigies conform to the same general layout as those illuminated by Pacino. The stave height of the music is the same; the framing of the illustration as a painting within a rectangular frame and the occasional addition of narrative roundels in the margin are consistent as well. In an illumination by the Master of the Dominican Effigies for Christmas Day (fig. 58) the scene of the Nativity dominates the page so completely that only three full words of the opening anthem—"Christo e na[to]" (Christ is born)—appear in alternating red and blue flourished initials below.

Unlike Pacino di Bonaguida, who was a lay citizen of Florence, Don Silvestro dei Gherarducci, author of the *Birth of the Virgin* miniature (fig. 47, and see also fig. 22) worked as an illuminator while serving as a monk. Born in Florence in 1339, he joined the Camaldolese order at age nine and took his monastic vows at thirteen. He is first mentioned as an illuminator of manuscripts at the monastery of Santa Maria degli Angeli in Florence almost two decades later, in 1370. By 1389 he was the subprior of the monastery, and in 1397, two years before his death, he was elected prior. Active as both a painter and a painter of manuscripts, Don Silvestro created illuminations only for his own monastery and for another Camaldolese house, San Michele a Murano.[83] In his *Lives of the Most Excellent Painters, Sculptors, and Architects* (1550), Vasari reported that Don Silvestro's work was so prized that after his death his fellow monks preserved his right hand, "which had labored so piously and so excellently for the service of sacred singing," as a relic.[84]

The Metropolitan's collection boasts two works for a choir book by the renowned Florentine painter Lorenzo Monaco: an illumination of the Last Judgment (fig. 59) and a preparatory drawing of Jesus Entering the Temple (fig. 60), both from the same ensemble of choir books for Santa Maria degli Angeli. Born Piero di Giovanni, Lorenzo took the name Lorenzo Monaco (Lawrence the Monk) when he joined the Camaldolese monastic community at Santa Maria degli Angeli in 1390, during the time that Don Silvestro was its subprior. Soon after he was made deacon in 1396 Lorenzo left the monastery to work on his own. He carried out commissions from his former monastery and from other ecclesiastical institutions, not only in Florence but also in Pisa. Active as an artist until 1424, he produced a body of work that though wide-ranging in scale and date is nonetheless remarkably consistent in figure style, palette, and compositional choices. His painting of Christ and the Virgin praying on behalf of a group of kneeling faithful (fig. 61), for example, measures some 94 inches in height, and a *Lamentation* by him (fig. 62) is only a little over 9 inches high. Yet his distinctive rendering of the lean, taut body of Christ is recognizable in both, as are the exquisite, chiseled features of the Virgin's profile and the figures' long, elegant fingers.

The life of Zanobi Strozzi, the illuminator of *King David in Prayer* (fig. 9), presents an atypical set of circumstances. Strozzi was an orphaned child from a celebrated aristocratic Florentine family, and

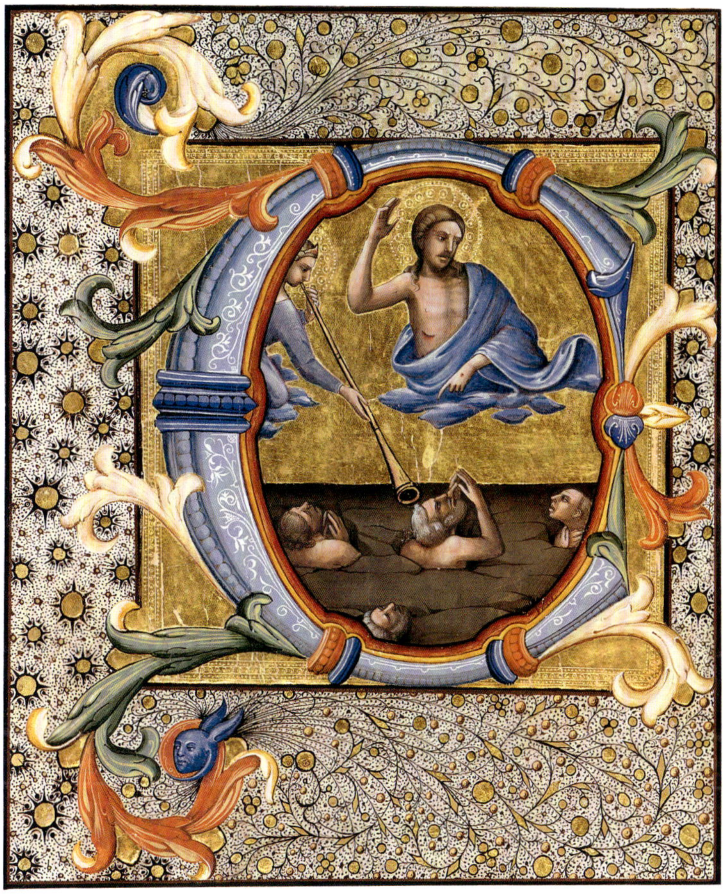

59. Lorenzo Monaco (documented 1391–1423/24). *Initial C with the Last Judgment.* Florence, ca. 1406–7. From an antiphonary created for the Camaldolese monastery of Santa Maria degli Angeli, Florence. Tempera, gold, and ink on parchment; 12 3/8 x 10 3/8 in. (31.3 x 26.4 cm). The Metropolitan Museum of Art, Robert Lehman Collection, 1975 (1975.1.2485)

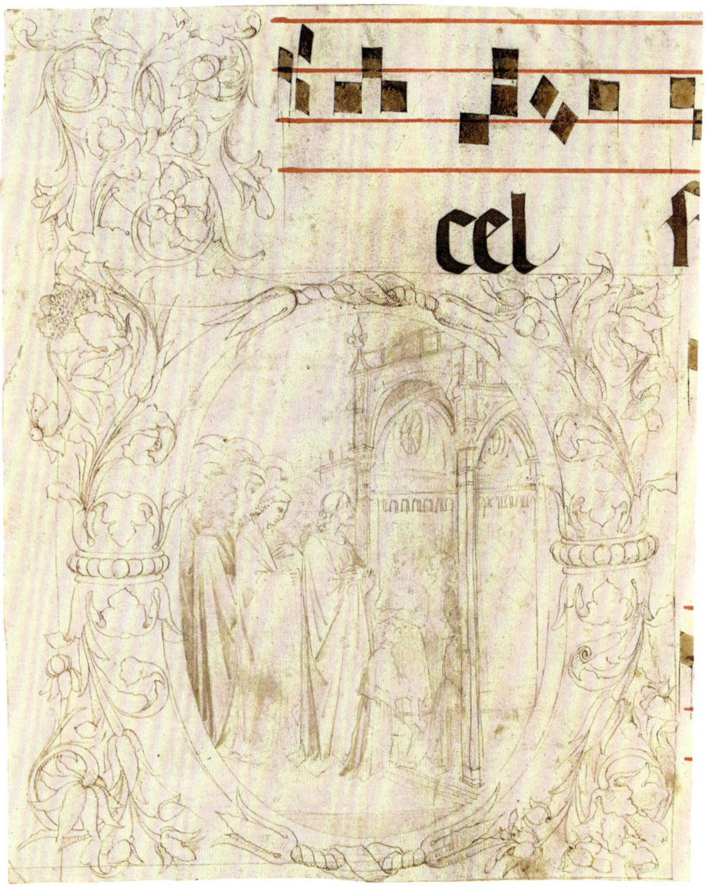


60. Lorenzo Monaco. *Initial D with Jesus Entering the Temple.* Florence, ca. 1408–11. From a gradual created for the Camaldolese monastery of Santa Maria degli Angeli, Florence. Pen and brown ink, brush and brown wash, over traces of leadpoint, on parchment; 12 x 9 1/2 in. (30.5 x 24.2 cm). The Metropolitan Museum of Art, Purchase, Lila Acheson Wallace Gift, 1999 (1999.391)

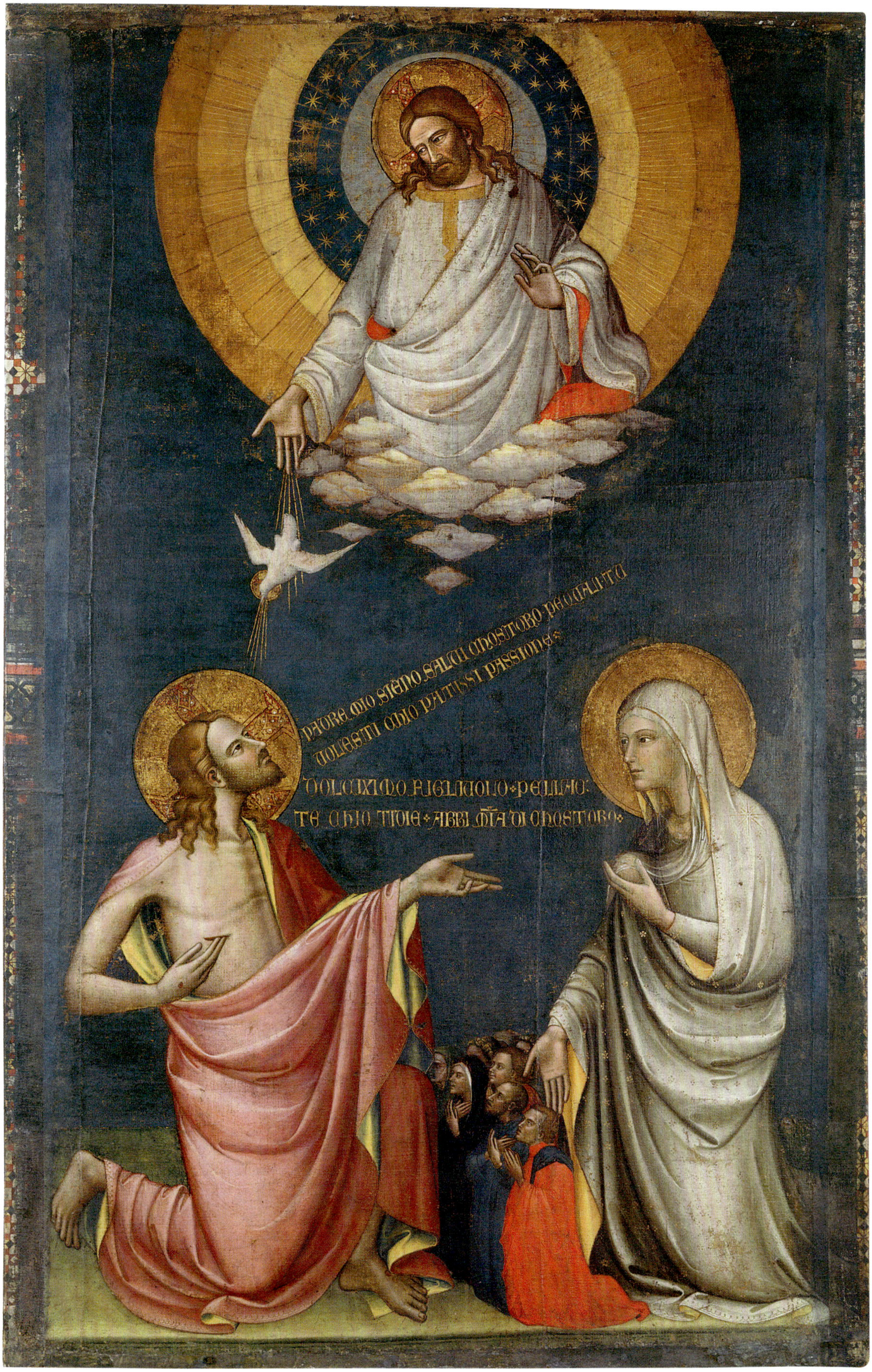


61. Lorenzo Monaco. *The Intercession of Christ and the Virgin*. Florence, before 1402. Tempera and gold on canvas; 94 ¼ x 60 ¼ x 1 in. (239.4 x 153 x 2.5 cm). The Metropolitan Museum of Art, The Cloisters Collection, 1953 (53.37)

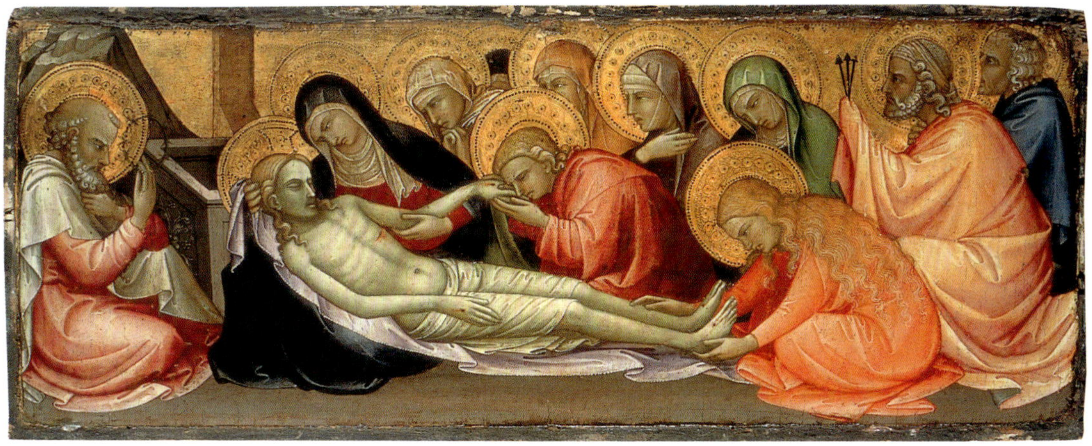

62. Lorenzo Monaco. *The Lamentation over the Dead Christ.* Florence, ca. 1404. Tempera and gold on panel, 9 3/8 x 23 5/8 in. (23.8 x 60.1 cm). Private collection

it has been suggested that his family's elevated status made him ineligible to join the Arte dei Medici e Speziali, or painters' guild, in Florence. Rather than serving as an apprentice, he was privately taught by an illuminator named Battista di Biagio Sanguigni, whom he ultimately supported in his dotage. In the mid-1440s Strozzi collaborated with Filippo di Matteo Torelli on a set of choir books for the monastery of San Marco in Florence.[85] Such division of labor was typical among illuminators.

A number of documents attest to the long and active career of the Florentine Mariano del Buono, who worked in the second half of the fifteenth century and to whom the large *Dedication of a Church* and *Funeral Procession* (figs. 54, 55) are attributed. In some records he is called a *cartolaio*, which most often signified a merchant involved in the supply and sale of materials for books and their bindings.[86] Elsewhere he is called *miniatore*, or miniature painter.[87] Mariano is documented as the illuminator of a breviary for the Hospital of Santa Maria Nuova in Florence, an antiphonary, and at least eight Hebrew manuscripts.[88] Among these is a diminutive prayer book in which a single Hebrew word rather than a single opening letter heralds the start of each new chapter (fig. 63). Images of prophets populate the margin of the prayer book, even at the center top, the place that in a Christian manuscript would have been understood as being reserved for an image of the deity.

Sano di Pietro's accomplishments are also well documented. Born in 1405, he was listed as a member of the painters' guild in his native Siena in 1428. The painter Sassetta, whose name appears above his in the members' roster, is thought to have been his teacher. In the space of two years in the 1440s Sano received commissions for three very distinct and important projects. In 1444 he is recorded as the painter of a large altarpiece, the following year he painted and signed a fresco in the Sala di Biccherna of the Palazzo Pubblico of Siena, and in 1446 he was paid for the illuminations, both historiated initials and decorated letters, for a psalter for Siena Cathedral. In addition to carrying out commissions for his native Siena, Sano worked for Olivetan monasteries, the Franciscans, the Augustinians, and Pope Pius II. After his death at age seventy-five he was buried in Siena's church of San Domenico, where his tombstone proclaimed him "a famous painter and completely dedicated to God."[89]

Sano di Pietro worked on the choir books of the Hospital of Santa Maria della Scala in Siena, the richest institution in Siena, located across the square from the cathedral in a building richly appointed with wall paintings celebrating its vital role as a charitable civic institution (figs. 64, 65). Coincident with the renovation of the hospital's church of the Most Holy Annunciation, the choir books were ordered by Niccolò Ricoveri, who was chosen by the town council to be rector of the hospital from 1456 to 1476. In Sano's *Initial D with the Martyrdom of Saint Agatha* (fig. 66), the saint, her beauty enhanced by the rosy vitality of her complexion and the delicious pink and green tonalities of her garment, seems unaffected by the excruciating and grotesque torture she is enduring. The Roman consul Quintianus sits watching as his minions carry out his orders that the young Christian martyr be tortured and her breasts cut off as punishment for rebuffing him.

Giovanni Pietro da Cemmo, creator of the limpid *Joseph Sold by His Brothers* (fig. 49, and see also figs. 50, 51), is documented between 1474 and 1507 as

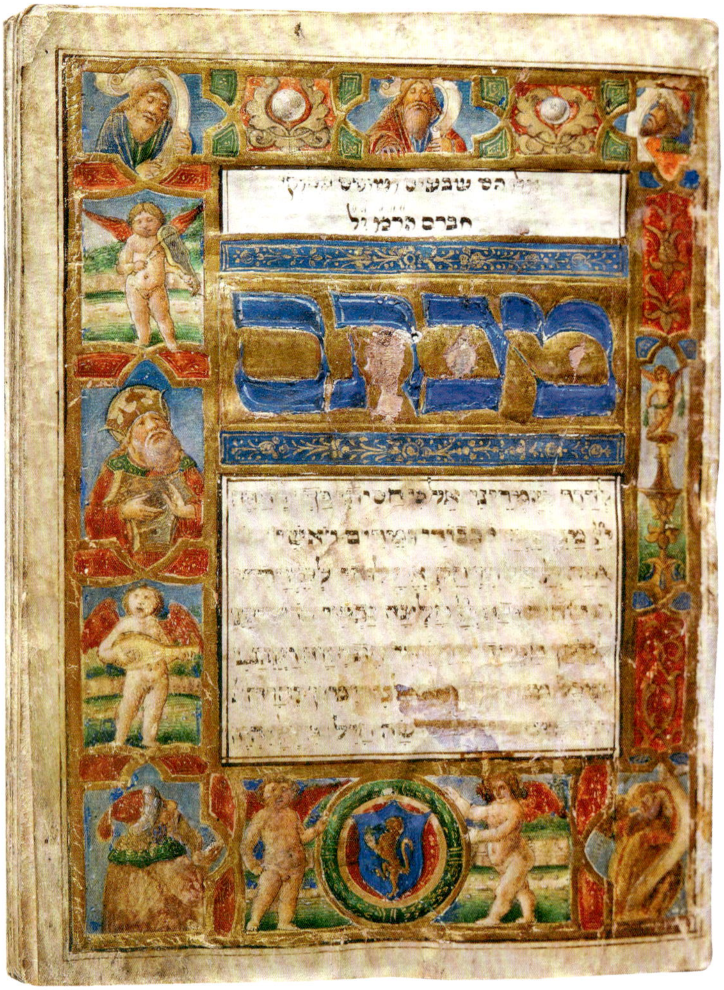

63. Mariano del Buono (1433–1504). Mahzor (prayer book). Florence, second half of 15th century. Tempera, gold, and ink on parchment; book 5 ⅞ x 4 ⅝ x 2 ⅜ in. (15 x 11.8 x 5.9 cm). The Library of The Jewish Theological Seminary, New York (Ms. 8641, fol. 1)

a fresco painter in Brescia and Cremona.[90] Stylistic evidence suggests that like Sano di Pietro and many other artists, including Fra Angelico, he was equally able as a manuscript illuminator. In fact, the pairing of these two media, so dissimilar in scale, seems to have been rather common in Italy.

The lively career of Belbello da Pavia differed markedly from that of Don Silvestro dei Gherarducci, the monk illuminator of Florence. Active from about 1430 to 1473, Belbello accepted commissions from the Church and also from members of the courts of Milan, Ferrara, and Mantua. He spent only about a year in Mantua before he was notoriously exiled in 1450 after being convicted of sodomy. By 1461 he was living in Pavia. Belbello's commission for the monastery of San Giorgio Maggiore in Venice, completed between 1467 and 1470, during the abbacy of Cipriano Rinaldini, included a volume with stunningly beautiful decorated initials that is now in The Cloisters. The figurative imagery has all been excised from the book and dispersed. A *Young Christ Blessing in an initial A* in the Getty Museum exemplifies Belbello's handsome half-length figures. To create an image of the young Jesus (fig. 67), he subtly modulated his otherwise sturdy and iconic images by using soft pink tones and painting delicate wisps of golden hair. But it is the narrative power of Belbello's work on the San Giorgio Maggiore choir books that is strongest, as seen in the *Annunciation* that served as the frontispiece to the Cloisters volume (fig. 68).[91] The urgency of the angel's message is suggested by his intent expression and taut, outstretched hand, the Virgin's

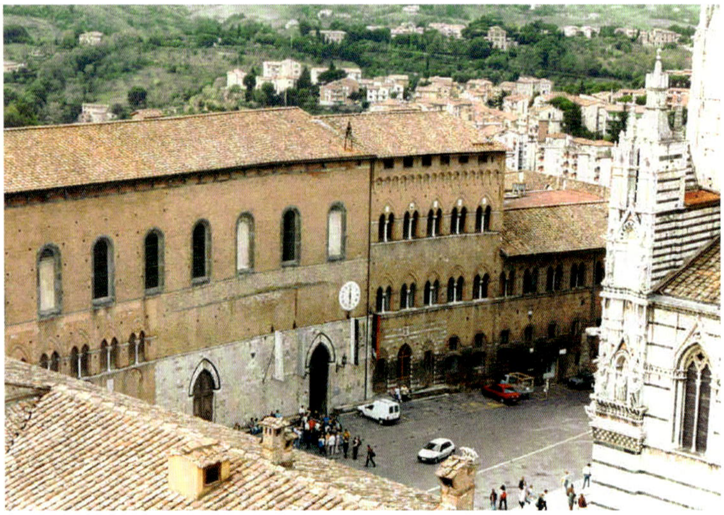

64. Hospital of Santa Maria della Scala, Siena

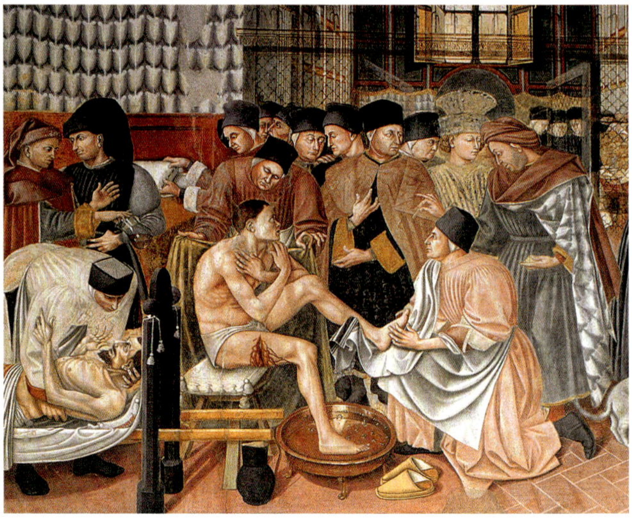

65. Domenico di Bartolo (ca. 1400–before 1445). *Care of the Sick* (detail). Siena, 1440–44. Fresco. Hospital of Santa Maria della Scala, Siena

reluctance by her tentative upward glance and curled fingers, while the upright of the letter M emphasizes the divide between them.

The training of the artists who decorated choir books followed no one particular pattern, and the inconsistent terminology in the documentation that survives can be misleading. Although some illuminators were taught in monasteries, following centuries-old tradition, they were not necessarily less innovative than those trained outside the Church. The case of the esteemed Don Silvestro offers ample evidence to the contrary. Some manuscript illuminators followed their forebears in well-established family businesses. Girolamo dai Libri's father, Francesco, was an illuminator, as was his grandfather, Stefano. Girolamo's name first appears in the record of a payment from the Olivetan monks of Santa Maria in Organo in Verona in 1495, and we know that he collaborated with his father in the creation of the choir books for the monastery (see figs. 7, 10). Still, despite the extensive documentation, and though Girolamo did sign panel paintings,[92] it is difficult definitively to attribute illuminations to him and to distinguish between his work and his father's, as the miniatures, with one exception that bears Francesco's name, are not signed.[93]

Although the scribe who provided the text of a manuscript often appended his name to his work, signed illuminations are rather uncommon. We know the name of the Bolognese illuminator Nerius (see figs. 42, 43) from his signature on a legal manuscript. (Bologna, with its great university, was renowned for the legal manuscripts produced there.) But Nerius is an exception, and despite scholars' continuing efforts to discern links between medieval documents and manuscripts, a substantial number

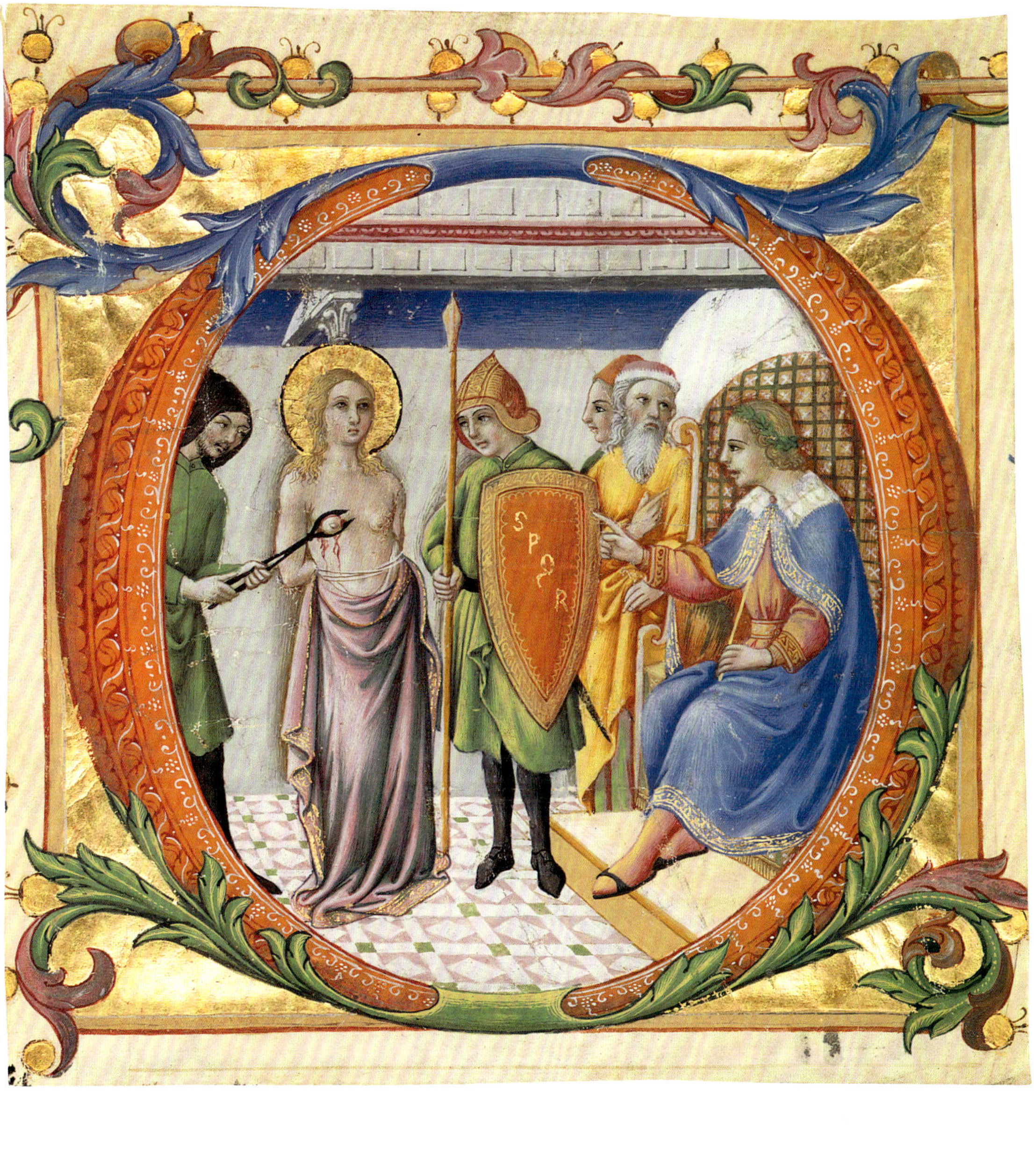


66. Sano di Pietro (1405–1481). *Initial D with the Martyrdom of Saint Agatha*. Siena, ca. 1470. From an antiphonary created for the Hospital of Santa Maria della Scala, Siena. Tempera, gold, and ink on parchment; 10⅜ x 10⅛ in. (26.3 x 25.7 cm). The Metropolitan Museum of Art, Robert Lehman Collection, 1975 (1975.1.2488)

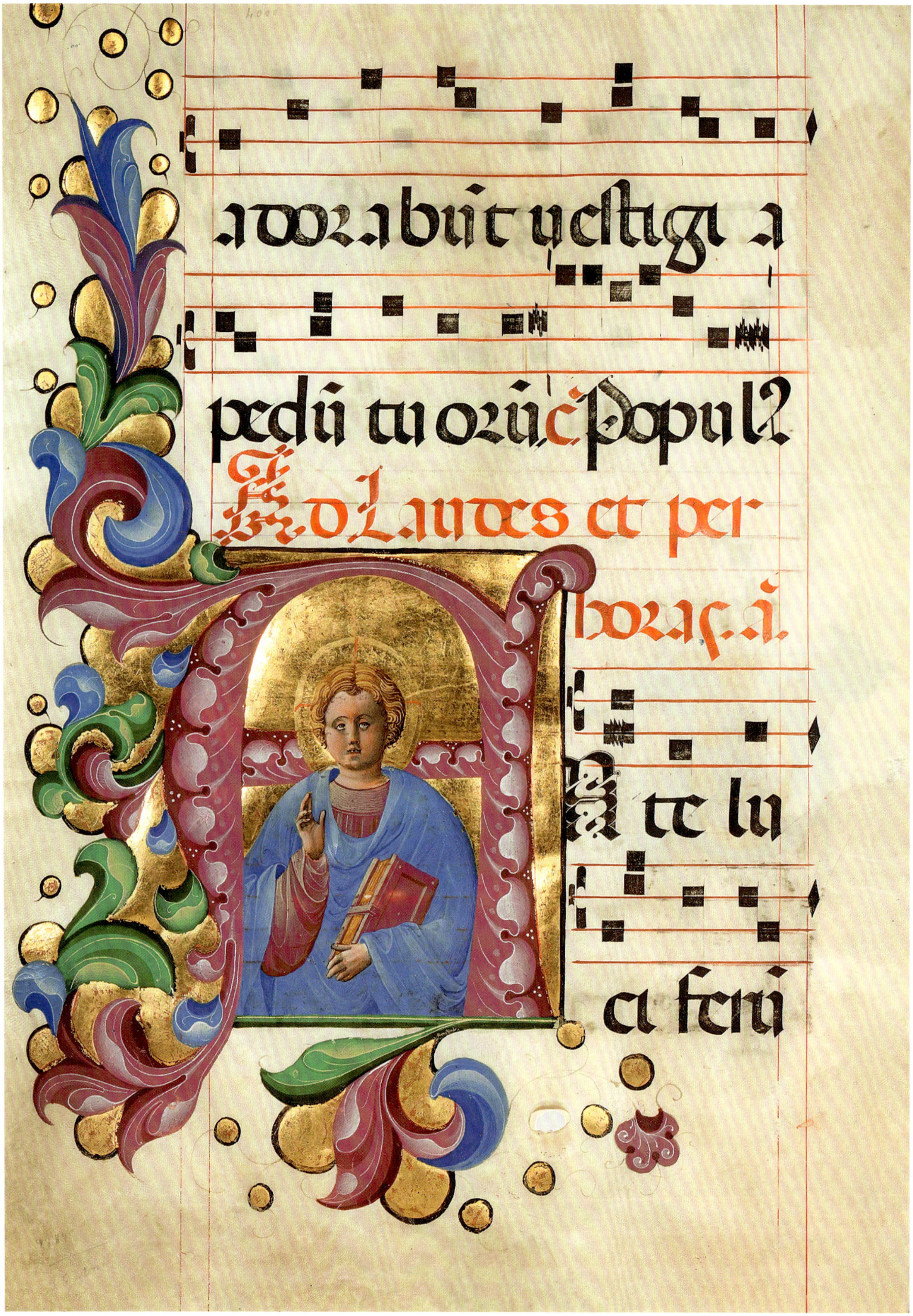


67. Belbello da Pavia. Leaf with *The Young Christ Blessing in an Initial A*. Venice, 1467–70. From an antiphonary created for the Benedictine monastery of San Giorgio Maggiore, Venice. Tempera, gold, and ink on parchment; 22 ½ x 16 in. (57.2 x 40.6 cm). The J. Paul Getty Museum, Los Angeles (2005.29.verso)

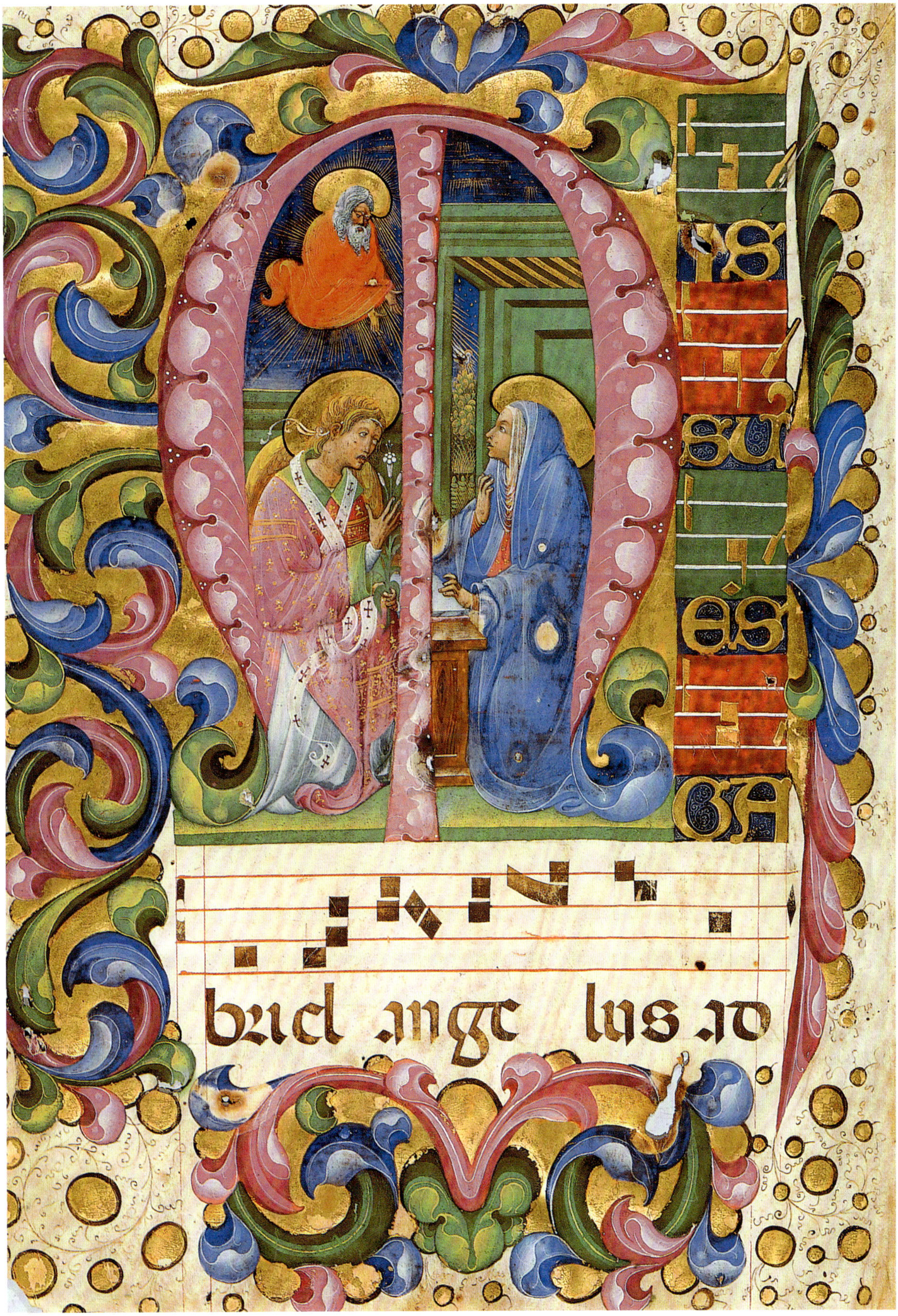


68. Belbello da Pavia. Leaf with *The Annunciation to the Virgin in an Initial M*. Venice, ca. 1467–70. From an antiphonary created for the Benedictine monastery of San Giorgio Maggiore, Venice. Tempera, gold, and ink on parchment; leaf 22 ½ x 15 ⅞ in. (57.2 x 40.4 cm). Fondazione Giorgio Cini, Venice (22093)

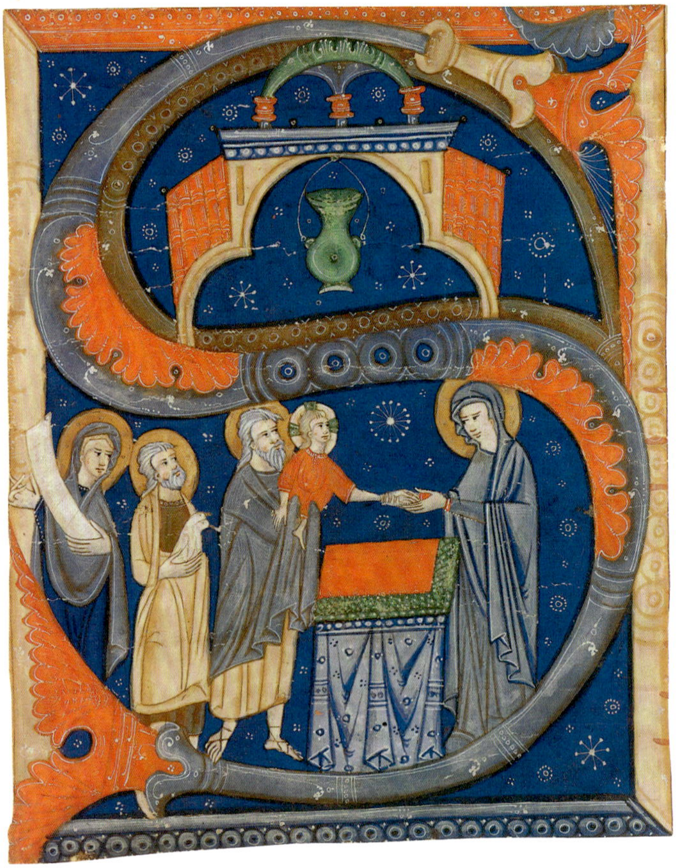

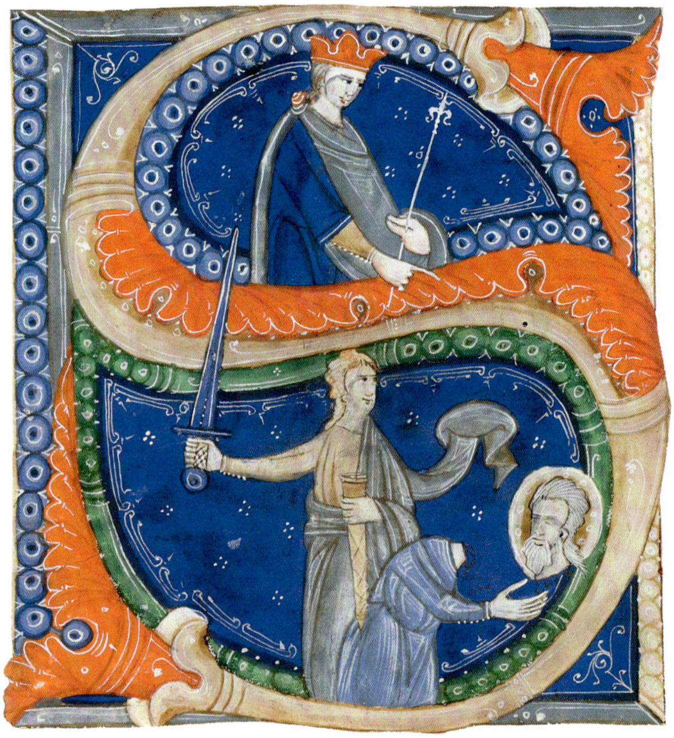

(above left)
69. Master of Bagnacavallo (active late 13th century). *Initial S with the Presentation of Christ in the Temple*. Imola, ca. 1278. From an antiphonary created for Imola Cathedral. Tempera and ink on parchment; 7 3/8 x 5 7/8 in. (18.6 x 14.9 cm). The Metropolitan Museum of Art, Gift of Bradish Johnson Carroll, 1926 (26.159.1)

(above right)
70. Master of Bagnacavallo. *Initial S with the Beheading of Saint Paul*. Imola, ca. 1278. From an antiphonary created for Imola Cathedral. Tempera and ink on parchment; 4 5/8 x 4 5/8 in. (11.8 x 11.8 cm). The Metropolitan Museum of Art, Gift of Bradish Johnson Carroll, 1926 (26.159.2)

of illuminators of Italian choir books still remain anonymous.

Even an artist whose hand can be recognized in a number of manuscripts may not yet have been matched with one of the numerous manuscript painters named in documents. The artist who illuminated one volume of a gradual preserved at the cathedral of Imola, near Bologna, must also have been responsible for two cuttings in the Metropolitan's collection (figs. 69, 70). The distinctive green hanging lamp, the figures' beady eyes and long fingers, and the background starburst pattern resembling fireworks on a field of blue are all hallmarks of his style. The manuscript in Imola, which covers the period from Palm Sunday through Pentecost, is believed to have been created for the new cathedral completed in 1271 and consecrated in 1278. Bishop Sinibaldo Meloti da Certaldo, who ordered the decoration of the tribune, may also have commissioned new choir books for the occasion.[94] Choir books were an integral part of the artistic and liturgical furnishings for a new or renovated church, chapel, or cathedral. The similarities between the illuminations of the Imola gradual (see fig. 71), attributed to an artist called the Master of Bagnacavallo, and the Metropolitan cuttings are strong enough to posit that our illuminations are from missing antiphonary volumes of the same set.

A fourteenth-century Bolognese illuminator known by scholars simply as the "Illustratore" seems to have been the author of the letter G with an image of a female saint (fig. 72), probably Dorothy, who is typically shown wearing a crown of roses. In addition to this illumination for a choir book, the Illustratore decorated numerous classical texts, including the *Digestum novum*, one volume of the ancient law code of Justinian (fig. 73). Characteristic of the illuminator's work are the elongated eyes, large strong nose, and muscular neck of the female figure set in a letter of deep blue highlighted with light touches of white penwork, including tiny diamond shapes and squiggles.

The *Initial M with the Annunciation* (fig. 5) in the Robert Lehman Collection at the Metropolitan has long been associated with the Maestro Daddesco, a prolific if largely anonymous artist active in Florence in the first half of the fourteenth century. The Maestro Daddesco was initially identified as a disciple of the early fourteenth-century Florentine painter Bernardo Daddi, and

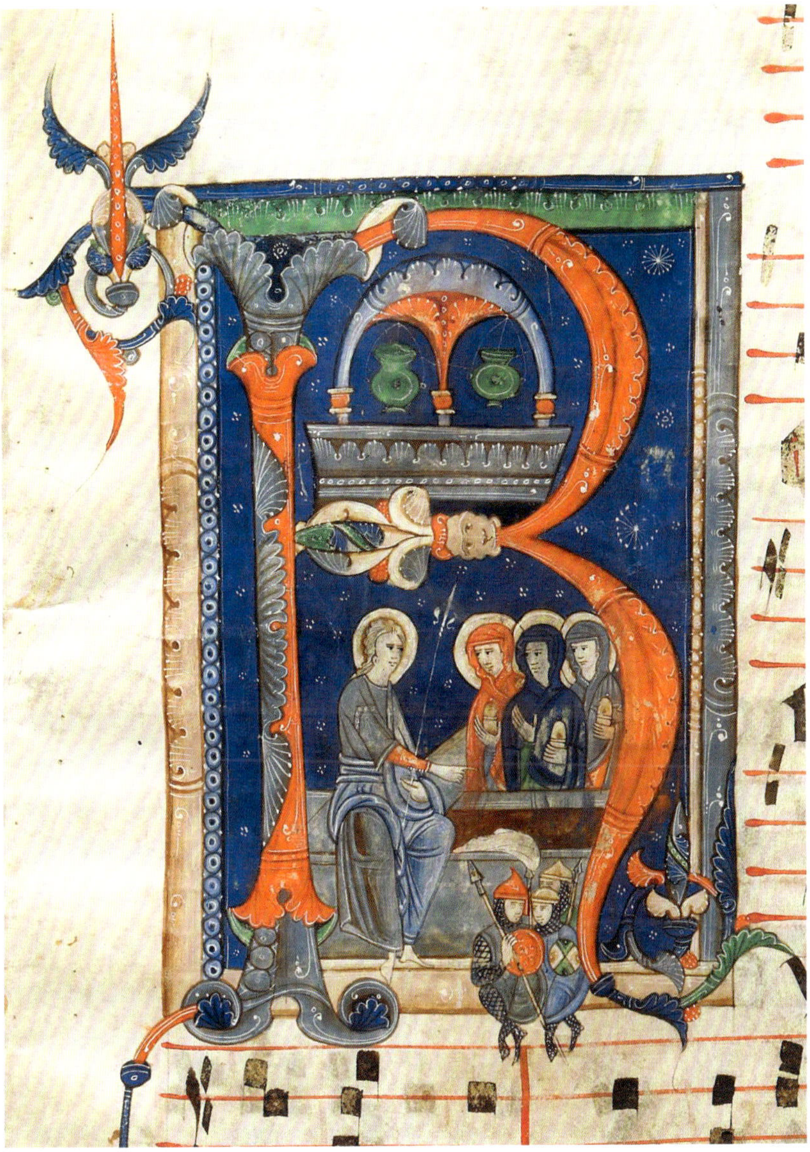

71. Master of Bagnacavallo. *Initial R with the Holy Women at the Tomb*. Imola, ca. 1278. From a gradual created for Imola Cathedral. Tempera and ink on parchment; book 20⅝ x 14⅜ in. (52.5 x 36.5 cm). Imola Cathedral (Graduale III, fol. 51r)

73. Attributed to the Illustratore. *Harvest Scene*. Bologna, 1330–47. From a copy of Justinian, *Digestum novum*. Tempera, gold, and ink on parchment; 5⅝ x 3 in. (14.4 x 7.6 cm). The J. Paul Getty Museum, Los Angeles (85.MS.213.verso)

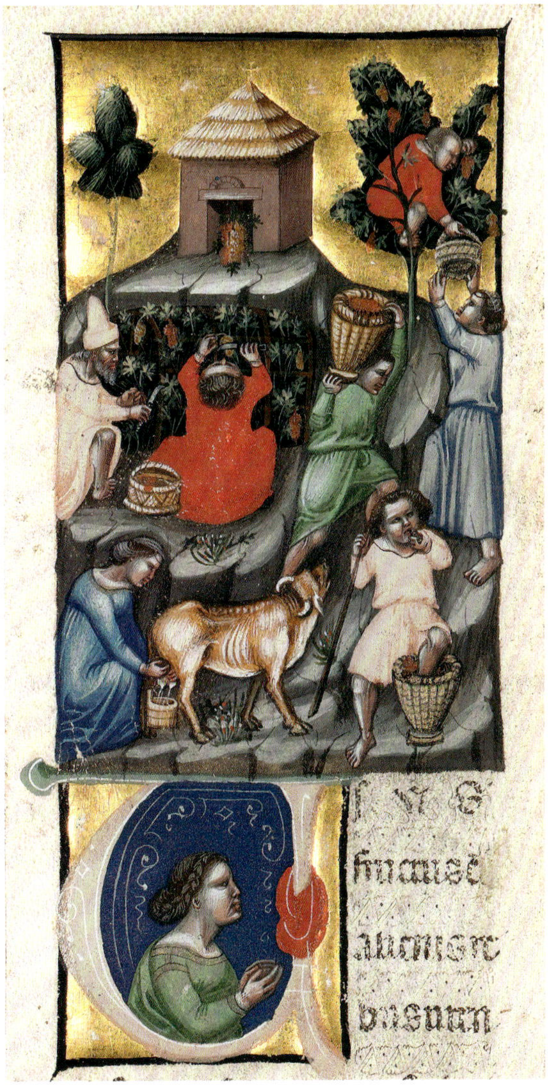

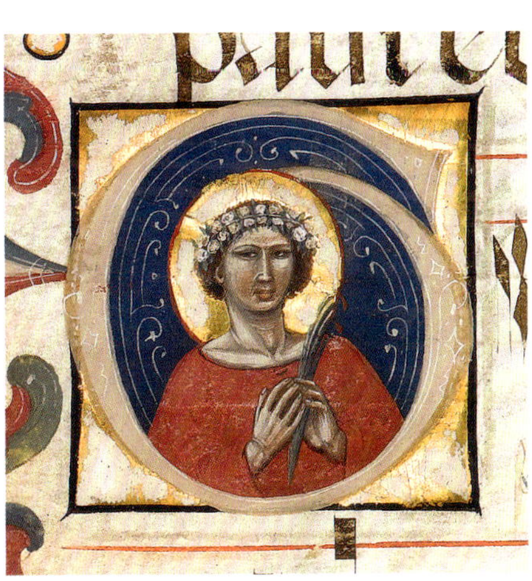

72. Attributed to the Illustratore (active 1330–74). Leaf from a gradual with *A Female Saint (Possibly Dorothy) in an Initial G* (detail). Bologna, ca. 1330–40. Tempera, gold, and ink on parchment; leaf 18¾ x 13⅝ in. (47.7 x 34.6 cm). The Metropolitan Museum of Art, Bequest of Gwynne M. Andrews, 1930 (31.134.7a)

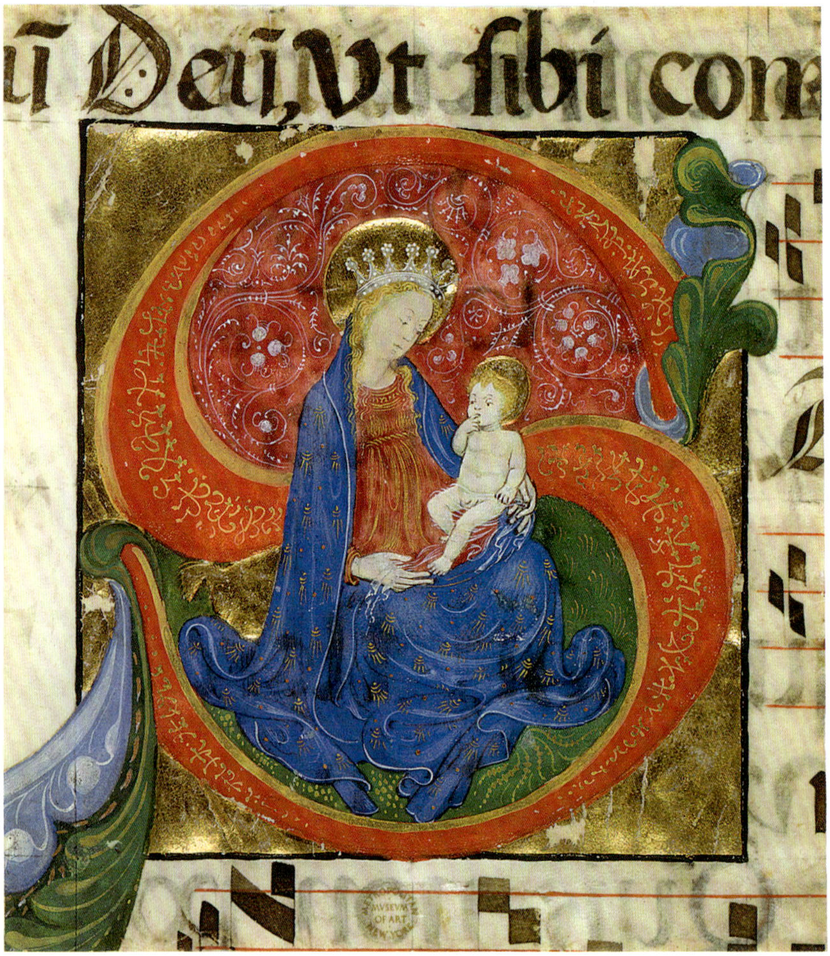

74. Master of the Franciscan Breviary (active ca. 1440–60). *Initial S with the Virgin and Child*. Lombardy, mid-15th century. From an antiphonary. Tempera, gold, and ink on parchment; 6 7/8 x 6 1/4 in. (17.6 x 15.8 cm). The Metropolitan Museum of Art, Rogers Fund, 1912 (12.56.2)

he has recently been linked to work carried out for the cathedral of Florence.[95] The specific context for the creation of the Lehman *Annunciation* remains unknown, however, and its authorship is unconfirmed.

The diaphanous drapery, the swirling floral ground, the delicate dusting with gold to suggest pattern and drapery folds, the tiny features of the figures, and the exotic patterning inspired by Arabic script mark the luxurious *Initial S with the Virgin and Child* (fig. 74) as the work of an artist known as the Master of the Franciscan Breviary. The master, who may have been a member of the Franciscan observants, created a number of choir books for Franciscan communities as far afield as Constantinople, and his work appears in manuscripts commissioned for Cardinal Ioannes Bessarion, papal legate and a renowned patron of manuscripts. Isolated initials by him can be found in a number of European and American collections.

The artist responsible for the *Initial O with Four Saints* (fig. 75) is called the Master of the Murano Gradual because of the provenance William Ottley gave the cutting, probably reliably, in the nineteenth century.[96] There is indeed a remarkable consonance between the presentation of these half-length figures and numerous other cuttings with images of saints now dispersed among a number of American and European museums (see fig. 76). Despite their common format, the images are painted with great care, with great variety in the attributes of individual saints or groups of saints. Two of the figures in the Metropolitan initial O are young and without readily identifiable attributes, but their two counterparts are dressed in the white robes of the Camaldolese order. The costumes, notably the cope decorated with red pomegranates, are rendered with great delicacy, and the penwork flourishes on the initial, again with a pattern inspired by Arabic lettering, are remarkable.

Whether their names have come down to us or not, illuminators of choir books were capable of creating works of considerable refinement. Again and again they painted with great subtlety that is sometimes only perceptible with thoughtful study at close range. Indeed, only under magnification (see fig. 77) can we perceive that the figures leading Mariano del Buono's funeral procession (fig. 55) actually have their mouths open in song.

The care they lavished on details is evident in the illuminators' work and also in the standards they set for themselves as members of guilds. For example, the Matricola dell'Arte dei Miniatori of Perugia, where a guild existed by 1310, not only legislated standards for the practice of their profession but also called for fines to be imposed, for instance if an artist tried to substitute azurite for lapis lazuli or stagno for silver.[97] Guaranteeing the consistent use of the best quality materials was essential to the good reputation of the guild, whether of illuminators, goldsmiths, or builders.[98]

There is a modern tendency to think of all works of art as the product of individual genius. The evidence from illuminated choir books offers a much more complicated picture. These were ambitious undertakings, often conceived as part of a larger program of enriching the church, and their completion depended on cooperative effort. The gradual for Santa Maria degli Angeli (see figs. 47, 60), for example, was part of a campaign that included a lectern and a cloth for the altar, all facilitated by the gift of one of the monks, Fra

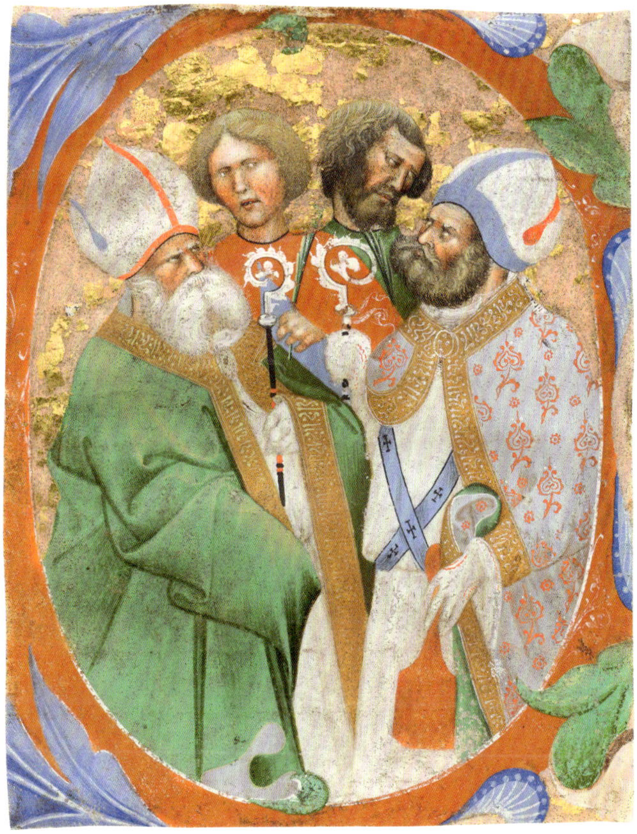

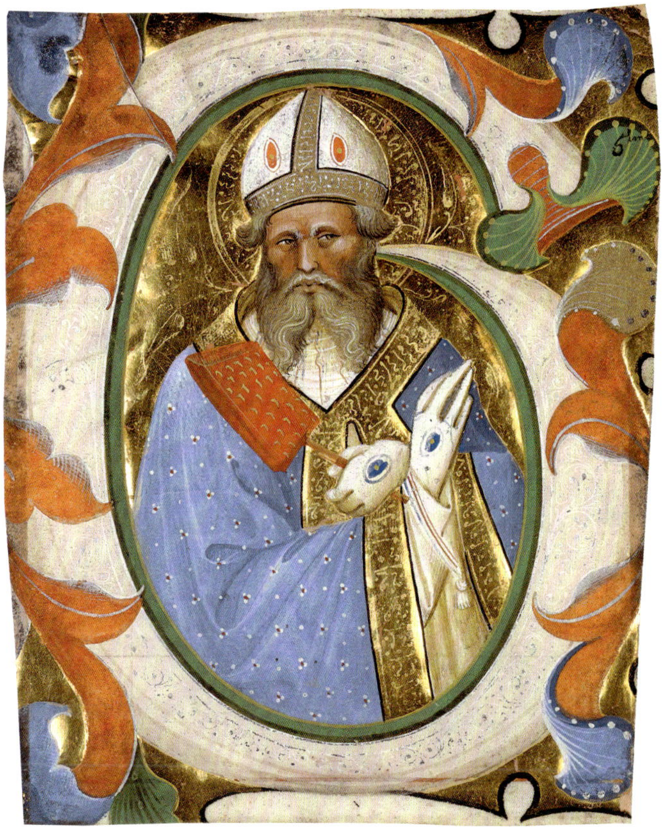

Leonardo, in honor of his deceased father.[99] The choir books that Cosimo de' Medici, grand duke of Tuscany, commissioned for San Marco in Florence were to be painted by Zanobi Strozzi, the author of the cutting with David in prayer (fig. 9). But the contract specified that Strozzi's work had to be checked by Fra Angelico and that Vespasiano da Bisticci was responsible for the bindings.[100]

The environment in which choir books were conceived was not entirely otherworldly. The books were sometimes commissioned by powerful political figures, and their illustrations, whether of the murder of Saint Peter Martyr or the Battle of the Maccabees (figs. 23, 24, 52), sometimes reflect the collision of the secular and sacred. In all instances, however, illuminated choir books celebrate life in community. In this they are distinct from books intended for private study or prayer. Almost by definition, therefore, they are boldly colored, large in size, and powerfully realized. In the Middle Ages they provided a visual spectacle to complement the music that filled the air. More surely than did notation to the music, painted illustrations offered meter and a rhythm to the book. The song heard on any given day and the image that accompanied it were unique to that occasion. In an era when every day was, literally, a holiday, choir books brought to each day its own sense of wonder.

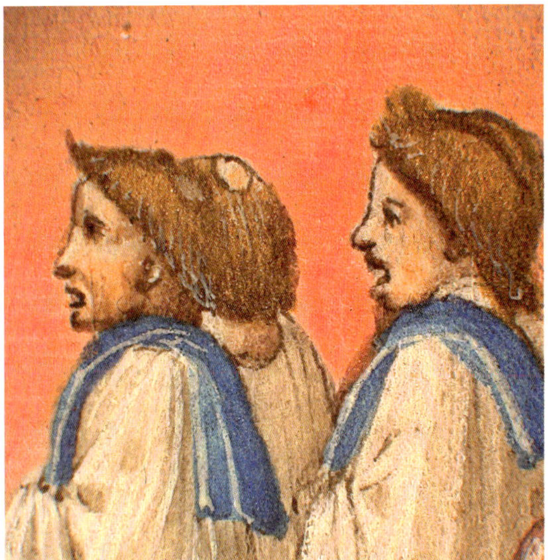

77. Photomicrograph of detail of fig. 55

(above left)
75. Master of the Murano Gradual (active ca. 1430–60). *Initial O with Four Saints*. Probably Veneto, 1440–50. From a Camaldolese choir book. Tempera, gold, and ink on parchment; 6 x 4 ¾ in. (15.2 x 11.9 cm). The Metropolitan Museum of Art, Rogers Fund, 1948 (48.40)

(above right)
76. Master of the Murano Gradual. *Initial G with Saint Blaise*. Venice, ca. 1450–60. From a gradual. Tempera, gold, and ink on parchment; 6 ⅛ x 4 ¾ in. (15.7 x 12 cm). The J. Paul Getty Museum, Los Angeles (2003.87.recto)

## The Italian Peninsula, ca. 1400

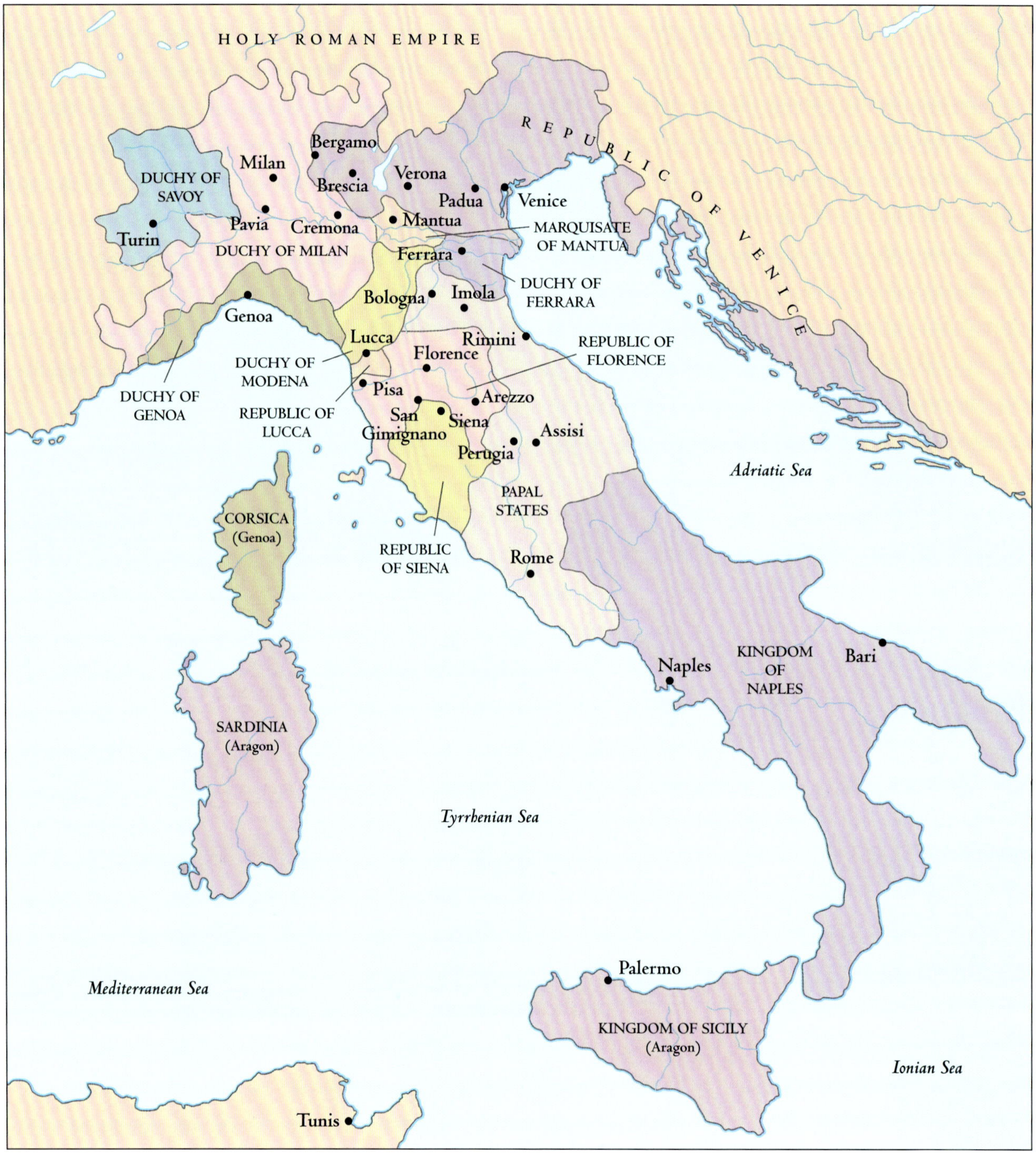

# Modern Italy

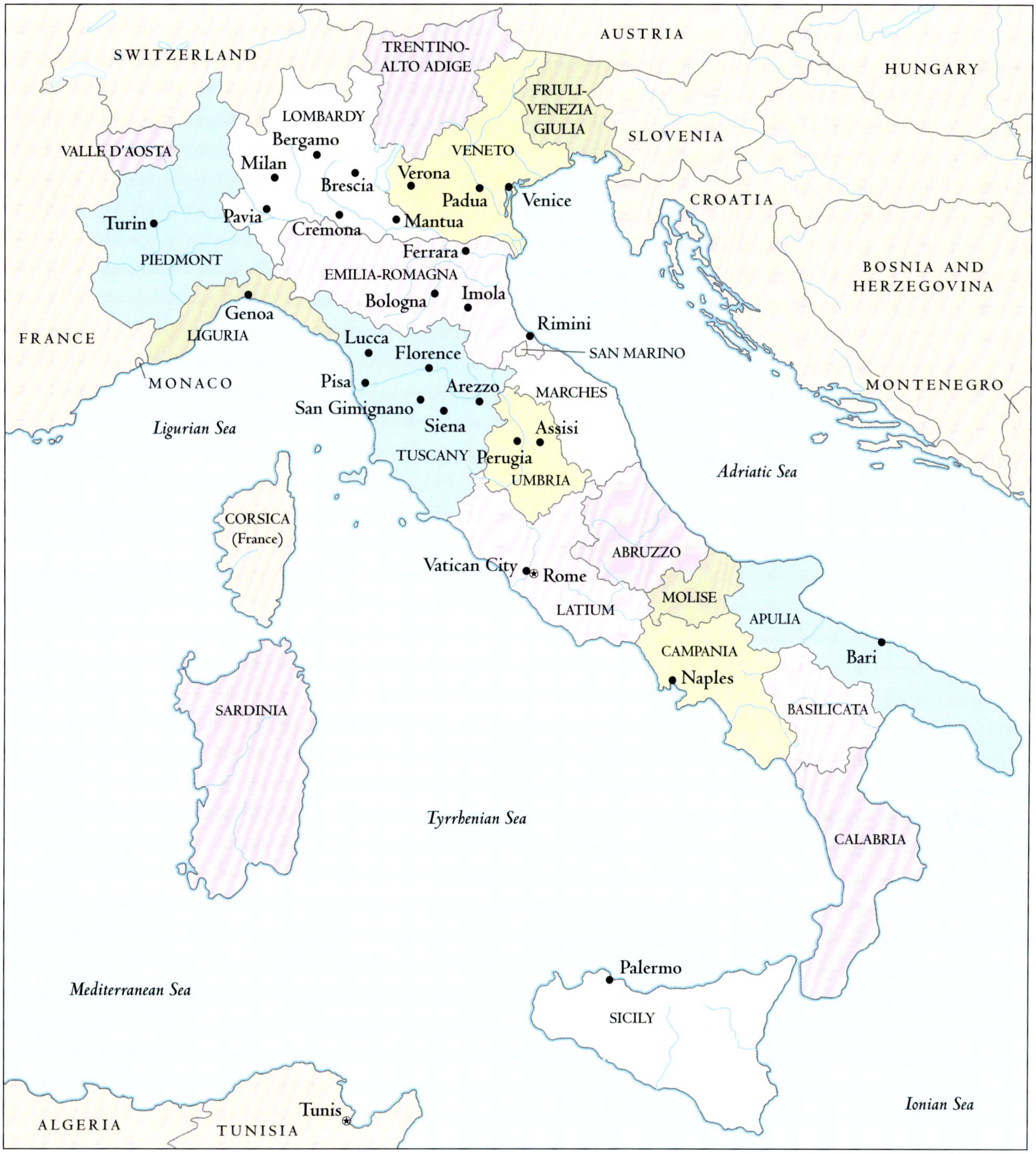

# Notes

All biblical citations are to the Douay-Rheims Version. Sources for quotations in headings. Page 7: Cassiodorus, *In psalterium praefatio*, in *Patrologiae latina*, vol. 70, p. 1; page 8: Hindman et al. 2001, p. 88; page 10: "The Exultet," a fifth- to seventh-century hymn used on Holy Saturday; page 12: Psalm 119:164; page 15: Pesce 1999, p. 419; page 16: Dante, *Purgatory* 16.18–20; page 20: Celotti sale 1825, p. 3; page 31: 1406 inventory of the library in Camaldoli, no. 15 (British Museum, MS Egerton 3036); page 33: Niceta of Remesiana, *De utilitate hymnorum* 13; page 37: Genesis 28:17; page 48: Dibdin 1817, vol. 1, note p. cxxv.

1. See Jacobi 1982.
2. Sacks 2007.
3. Tacconi 2003.
4. De la Mare 1985, p. 409.
5. Tacconi 2005, pp. 38–39, and appendix B.
6. Vasari (1550) 1906, vol. 2 pp. 22–23. See the account by Laurence B. Kanter in Kanter et al. 1994, pp. 229–34.
7. Ciliberti 1994, pp. 51–70.
8. Ciardi Duprè dal Poggetto 1972.
9. Celotti sale 1825, p. 3, quoted in Munby 1972, p. 67.
10. Dibdin 1817, vol. 1, pp. cxii–cxiii.
11. Freuler 1997, pp. 276, 353.
12. Munby 1972, p. 158.
13. Quoted in Hindman et al. 2001, p. 88.
14. Dibdin 1817, vol. 1, p. cxii.
15. Munby 1972, p. 65.
16. See Benevolo and Medica 2003, p. 146.
17. See ibid., pp. 145–59.
18. Ciliberti 1994, p. 84.
19. Strohm 1993, p. 321.
20. Cited in Tacconi 2005, p. 8n1.
21. Tacconi 1999, pp. 226–27; Fabbri and Tacconi 1997, pp. 216–17.
22. The discussion of psalmody in Jewish tradition depends on research conducted by Rachel Travis under Vivian B. Mann's and my direction for her M.A. in Jewish Art at the Jewish Theological Seminary in New York.
23. Schleifer 1992, pp. 20–21.
24. I am grateful to Rachel Travis and Vivian B. Mann for this research. See also McKinnon 1979–80.
25. See McKinnon 1987, pp. 12–17; Smith 1984; and Fassler and Jeffery 1992, pp. 84–85.
26. Pliny, *Letters*, trans. Betty Radice, Loeb Classical Library, no. 59 (Cambridge, Mass., 1969), vol. 2, book 10, letter xcvi, pp. 402–5; translated in McKinnon 1987, p. 27.
27. Tertullian, *Ad uxorem*, 2.8.8–9, in *Patrologiae latina*, vol. 1, col. 1304.
28. James W. McKinnon, "Christian Church, Music of the Early, I, 4i: Psalmody and the Developing Office," *Grove Music Online, Oxford Music Online*, www.oxfordmusiconline.com.
29. De Capoa 2003, p. 215. See I Kings 16:16–23 and I Chronicles 15:15–29.
30. "Life of Saint Antony, 44," in *Patrologiae graeca*, vol. 26, col. 908; translated in McKinnon 1987, p. 55, no. 105.
31. Cited by McKinnon in *Grove Music Online*. I am grateful to Rachel Travis for bringing these citations by McKinnon to my attention.
32. "Homilia in psalmum 1, 2," in *Patrologiae graeca*, vol. 29, col. 212; McKinnon 1987, pp. 65–66, no. 131.
33. Jeffery 1984.
34. Saint Benedict, *Rule for Monasteries*, trans. L. Doyle (1948), p. 40.
35. Cassiodorus, *In psalterium praefatio*, in *Patrologiae latina*, vol. 70, p. 1.
36. David Hiley and Janka Szendrei, "Notation, III, 1: History of Western Notation: Plainchant I, iii: Origins and Earliest Examples," *Grove Music Online*.
37. Carpenter 1958, p. 16.
38. Boynton 1997, pp. 8, 44.
39. See James W. McKinnon, "Gregorian Chant," *Grove Music Online*, and Levy 1987.
40. This is the position advanced by Levy 1987, pp. 10–11. The interpretation of the term *notas* in the lists of school requirements as "notes" has been the subject of some discussion; there is no question that *cantus* (chants) are included, appearing in sequence just after *notas*. Hiley (1993, p. 297) argues against the existence of a Carolingian exemplar for notation. At the time there may have been dialogue between Carolingian and Byzantine musicians, but notation developed differently in the Orthodox tradition. Byzantine chant was also not typically notated in the eighth century.
41. Translated in Levy 1998, p. 185.
42. Translated by Boynton 1997, p. 219. For the fiery furnace, see Daniel 3:13–100.
43. I am grateful to Vivian B. Mann and Rachel Travis for bringing this to my attention. See Gold 1967.
44. Pesce 1999, p. 417.
45. Ibid., p. 419.
46. Tacconi 2005, pp. 39–42.
47. See note 36 above.
48. *Grove Music Online* is the most useful reference. This particular information comes from the discussion "Gradual: Origins and Early History." Elsewhere, McKinnon (2001, p. 686) cites the number of chants in the Roman Proper of the Mass at more than 550, including about 150 introits, 100 graduals, 50 alleluias, 95 offertories, and 150 communion hymns, as well as 20 tracts, occasionally substituted for alleluias in times of penance.
49. See Alexander 1994, p. 227, no. 121.
50. Ilnitchi 2001, p. 657.
51. Hiley 1993, p. 305. Antiphons for the Benedictus and Magnificat are sometimes bound in a separate volume as well.
52. "Music in Dante's 'Divine Comedy'" 1895, pp. 446–48; Stillman 2005.
53. Dante, *Purgatory* 16.18–20.
54. Celotti sale 1825, p. 3, cited by Munby 1972, pp. 65, 67.
55. See Bonniwell 1945, and Hinnebusch 1965, pp. 347–49.
56. Baroffio 2006, p. 35.
57. Levy 1974, p. 206.
58. Ciliberti 1994, pp. 71–72.
59. See Humphreys 1964.
60. Suggested by Giordana Mariani Canova, following an earlier suggestion by Laurence Kanter linking the cuttings to the Franciscan convento of Corpus Domini at Ferrara. See the summary of arguments by Federica Toniolo in Natale et al. 2007, pp. 304–5, no. 61.
61. See Lugano 1911, and *Codici liturgici miniati* 1982, pp. 37–40.
62. Marinelli and Marini 2006, pp. 379–81, no. 125a–d.
63. Vasari (1550) 1906, vol. 2, p. 24.
64. I am grateful to Dirk H. Breiding, assistant curator in the Department of Arms and Armor at the Metropolitan, for the description of the armor. He points out that the two-part construction of the breastplate went out of fashion about 1500.
65. The arms do not correspond to those of the abbot of Vallombrosa. I am grateful to R. Theo Margelony, departmental coordinator, Medieval Art, at the Metropolitan, for blazoning the arms. I thank Helmut Nickel for his advice on both the armor and the arms.
66. Webster 1908.
67. D'Accone 1997, pp. 171–72.
68. Ciliberti 1994, p. 60.
69. See Alexander 1978.
70. Dibdin 1817, p. cxiii.
71. Niccolò di ser Sozzo was probably the son of the Sienese illuminator Ser Sozzo di Stefano, who is documented from 1293 to 1321 (see Moran and Fineschi 1976). However, some scholars do not support this theory.
72. D'Accone 1997, p. 91.
73. I am grateful to Reverend John Perris for clarifying the relationships between the characters for me.
74. See Mariani Canova 1992, p. 167, fig. 14.
75. Noted by Gaudenz Freuler in Kanter et al. 1994, p. 150, no. 16h.
76. Noted by Frizzell and Henderson 2001, p. 194. See *Rationale Divinorum Officiorum*, book 6, chap. 32.12.
77. For the origins of this tradition, see Dunbabin 1985.
78. Frick 2002, p. 89.
79. Weissman 1982, p. 43.
80. Children were also taught the devotional hymns, and *laude* remained part of popular Italian religious music into the nineteenth century.
81. On Pacino, see Kanter in Kanter et al. 1994, pp. 44–45.
82. As proposed by Kanter (ibid., p. 44).
83. See the summary of his career by Freuler in Kanter et al. 1994, pp. 124–26, and Freuler 1997.
84. Vasari (1550) 1906, vol. 2, p. 23n2.
85. See Levi D'Ancona in Hindman et al. 1997, p. 169, with earlier literature.
86. See de la Mare 1976, pp. 239–45, with earlier literature.
87. Levi D'Ancona 1962, pp. 175–81.
88. See Cohen, forthcoming.
89. Christiansen in Christiansen, Kanter, and Strehlke 1988, p. 138: "pictor famosius et homo totus deditus Deo."
90. See Marubbi 1992.
91. The reconstruction was first made by Palladino (2003).
92. See ibid., pp. 114–22, with earlier literature.
93. Castiglione 2008.
94. Lollini 2000, pp. 169–70; Faranda 1994, pp. 17–18, 178–80.
95. Tacconi 2000.
96. See note 9 above.
97. Subbioni 2006, p. 93.
98. For this theme in documentation concerning manuscript illumination, see Alexander 1992, p. 63.
99. See Freuler in Kanter et al. 1994, p. 131; Freuler 1997.
100. See Carl B. Strehlke in Kanter et al. 1994, p. 349.

# Bibliography


Alexander, Jonathan J. G. *The Decorated Letter*. New York, 1978.

———. *Medieval Illuminators and Their Methods of Work*. New Haven, 1992.

———, as ed. *The Painted Page: Italian Renaissance Book Illumination, 1450–1550*. Exh. cat., Royal Academy of Arts, London; Pierpont Morgan Library, New York. London and Munich, 1994.

Baroffio, Giacomo. "Liturgia e musica nella tradizione domenicana." In *Canto e colore: I corali di San Domenico di Perugia nella Biblioteca comunale Augusta (XIII–XIV sec.)*, edited by Claudia Parmeggiani, pp. 33–68. Exh. cat., Unicredit Banca, Perugia. Perugia, 2006.

Benevolo, Giancarlo, and Massimo Medica. *I corali di San Giacomo Maggiore: Miniatori e committenti a Bologna nel Trecento*. Exh. cat., Museo Civico Medievale. Bologna, 2003.

Bonniwell, William R. *A History of the Dominican Liturgy, 1215–1945*. New York, 1945.

Boynton, Susan Leslie. "Glossed Hymns in Eleventh-Century Continental Hymnaries." Ph.D. diss., Brandeis University, Waltham, Mass., 1997.

Carpenter, Nan Cooke. *Music in the Medieval and Renaissance Universities*. Norman, Okla., 1958.

Castiglioni, Gino, ed., with Gianni Peretti. *Per Girolamo dai Libri: Pittore e miniatore del Rinascimento veronese*. Exh. cat., Museo di Castelvecchio, Verona. Venice, 2008.

Celotti sale. *A Catalogue of a Highly Valuable and Extremely Curious Collection of Illumined Miniature Paintings . . . Taken from the Choral Books of the Papal Chapel in the Vatican, during the French Revolution; and Subsequently Collected and Brought to This Country by the Abate Celotti*. Sale cat. by William Young Ottley. Mr. Christie, London, May 26, 1825.

Christiansen, Keith, Laurence B. Kanter, and Carl Brandon Strehlke. *Painting in Renaissance Siena, 1420–1500*. Exh. cat., MMA. New York, 1988.

Ciardi Duprè dal Poggetto, M. G. *I Corali del Duomo di Siena*. Siena, 1972.

Giliberti, Galliano. *Musica e liturgia nelle chiese e conventi dell'Umbria (secoli X–XV)*. Perugia, 1994.

*Codici liturgici miniati dei Benedettini in Toscana*. Exh. cat., Centro d'Incontro della Certosa del Galluzzo, Florence. Florence, 1982.

Cohen, Evelyn M. "A Woman's Hebrew Prayer Book and the Art of Mariano del Buono." In *Between Judaism and Christianity: Art-Historical Essays in Honor of Elisheva (Elisabeth) Revel Neher*, edited by Katrin Kogman-Appel and Mati Meyer. Leiden: E. J. Brill, forthcoming 2009.

D'Accone, Frank A. *The Civic Muse: Music and Musicians in Siena during the Middle Ages and the Renaissance*. Chicago, 1997.

De Capoa, Chiara. *Old Testament Figures in Art*. Los Angeles, 2003.

Dibdin, Thomas F., Rev. *The Bibliographical Decameron; or, Ten Days Pleasant Discourse upon Illuminated Manuscripts and Subjects Connected with Early Engraving, Typography, and Bibliography*. 3 vols. London, 1817.

Dunbabin, Jean. "The Maccabees as Exemplars in the Tenth and Eleventh Centuries." In *The Bible in the Medieval World: Essays in Memory of Beryl Smalley*, edited by Katherine Walsh and Diana Wood, pp. 31–41. London, 1985.

Fabbri, Lorenzo, and Marica Tacconi. *I libri del Duomo di Firenze: Codici liturgici e Biblioteca di Santa Maria del Fiore (secoli XI–XVI)*. Exh. cat., Biblioteca Medicea Laurenziana di Firenze. Florence, 1997.

Faranda, Franco, ed. *Cor unum et anima una: Corali miniati della Chiesa di Imola*, Faenza, 1994.

Fassler, Margot, and Peter Jeffery. "Christian Liturgical Music from the Bible to the Renaissance." In *Sacred Sound and Social Change: Liturgical Music in Jewish and Christian Experience*, edited by Lawrence A. Hoffman and Janet R. Walton, pp. 84–123. Notre Dame, Ind., 1992.

Freuler, Gaudenz. *Tendencies of Gothic in Florence: Don Silvestro dei Gherarducci*. Vol. 7, part 2 of *A Critical and Historical Corpus of Florentine Painting*, section IV. Edited by Miklos Boskovits. Florence, 1997.

Frick, Carole Collier. *Dressing Renaissance Florence: Families, Fortunes, and Fine Clothing*. Baltimore, 2002.

Frizzell, Lawrence E., and J. Frank Henderson. "Jews and Judaism in the Medieval Latin Liturgy." In *The Liturgy of the Medieval Church*, edited by Thomas J. Heffernan and E. Ann Matter. Kalamazoo, Mich., 2001.

Gold, Norman. "The Music of Obadiah the Proselyte and His Conversion." *Journal of Jewish Studies* 18 (1967), pp. 43–63.

Hiley, David. *Western Plainchant: A Handbook*. Oxford, 1993.

Hindman, Sandra, et al. *The Robert Lehman Collection, IV: Illuminations*. Contributions by Mirella Levi D'Ancona, Pia Palladino, and Maria Francesca Saffiotti. New York: MMA, 1997.

———. *Manuscript Illumination in the Modern Age: Recovery and Reconstruction*. Contributions by Michael Camille, Nina Rowe, and Rowan Watson. Exh. cat., Mary and Leigh Block Museum of Art, Northwestern University, Evanston. Evanston, Ill., 2001.

Hinnebusch, William A. *The History of the Dominican Order*. Vol. 1, *Origins and Growth to 1500*. New York, 1965.

Humphreys, K. W. *The Book Provisions of the Mediaeval Friars, 1215–1400*. Amsterdam, 1964.

Ilnitchi, Gabriela. "Music in the Liturgy." In *The Liturgy of the Medieval Church*, edited by Thomas J. Heffernan and E. Ann Matter, pp. 645–71. Kalamazoo, Mich., 2001.

Jacobi, Peter. *The Messiah Book: The Life and Times of G. F. Handel's Greatest Hit*. New York, 1982.

Jeffery, Peter. "The Introduction of Psalmody into the Roman Mass by Pope Celestine I (422–432)." *Archiv für Liturgiewissenschaft* 26 (1984), pp. 147–65.

Kanter, Laurence B., Barbara Drake Boehm, Carl Brandon Strehlke, Gaudenz Freuler, Christa C. Mayer Thurman, and Pia Palladino. *Painting and Illumination in Early Renaissance Florence, 1300–1450*. Exh. cat., MMA. New York, 1994.

Levi D'Ancona, Mirella. *Miniatura e miniatori a Firenze dal XIV al XVI secolo: Documenti per la storia della miniatura*. Florence, 1962.

Levy, Kenneth. "A Dominican Organum Duplum." *Journal of the American Musicological Society* 27, no. 2 (Summer 1974), pp. 183–211.

———. "Charlemagne's Archetype of Gregorian Chant." *Journal of the American Musicological Society* 40, no. 1 (Spring 1987), pp. 1–30.

———. *Gregorian Chant and the Carolingians*. Princeton, 1998.

Lollini, Fabrizio, ed. *Corali miniati di Faenza, Bagnacavallo e Cotignola: Tesori dalla Diocesi*. Exh. cat., Centro Culturale "Le Cappuccine," Bagnacavallo. Faenza, 2000.

Lugano, Placido. "Il primo corpo di Costituzioni monastiche per l'Ordine di Monteoliveto." *Rivista storica benedettina* 6 (1911), pp. 107–34.

McKinnon, James W. "The Exclusion of Musical Instruments from the Ancient Synagogue." *Proceedings of the Royal Music Association* 106 (1979–80), pp. 77–87.

———. *Music in Early Christian Literature*. Cambridge, 1987.

———. "Gregorius Presul Composuit Hunc Libellum Musicae Artis." In *The Liturgy of the Medieval Church*, edited by Thomas J. Heffernan and E. Ann Matter, pp. 673–94. Kalamazoo, Mich., 2001.

de la Mare, Albina C. "Bartolomeo Scala's Dealings with Booksellers, Scribes, and Illuminators, 1459–63, II: The Book Trade." *Journal of the Warburg and Courtauld Institutes* 39 (1976), pp. 239–45.

———. "New Research on Humanistic Scribes in Florence." In *Miniatura fiorentina del Rinascimento, 1440–1525: Un primo censimento*, edited by Annarosa Garzelli, vol. 1. Florence, 1985.

Mariani Canova, Giordana. "La miniatura degli ordini mendicanti nell'arco adriatico all'inizio del trecento." In *Arte e spiritualità negli ordini mendicanti: Gli Agostiniani e il cappellone di San Nicola a Tolentino*. Rome, 1992.

Marinelli, Sergio, and Paola Marini, eds. *Mantegna e le arti a Verona, 1450–1500*. Exh. cat., Palazzo della Gran Guardia, Verona. Venice, 2006.

Marubbi, Mario. "Giovan Pietro da Cemmo miniatore." *Arte lombarda* 101, no. 2 (1992), pp. 7–31.

Moran, Gordon, and Sonia Fineschi. "Niccolò di Ser Sozzo—Tegliacci or di Stefano?" *Paragone arte* 27, no. 321 (November 1976), pp. 58–63.

Munby, A. N. L. *Connoisseurs and Medieval Miniatures, 1750–1850*. Oxford, 1972.

"Music in Dante's 'Divine Comedy.'" *Musical Times and Singing Class Circular*, vol. 36, no. 629 (July 1, 1895), pp. 446–48.

Natale, Mauro, et al. *Cosmè Tura e Francesco del Cossa, L'arte a Ferrara nell'età di Borso d'Este*. Exh. cat., Palazzo dei Diamanti and Palazzo Schifanoia, Ferrara. Ferrara, 2007.

Palladino, Pia. *Treasures of a Lost Art: Italian Manuscript Painting of the Middle Ages and Renaissance*. Exh. cat., Cleveland Museum of Art; Fine Arts Museums of San Francisco; MMA, New York, 2003.

Pesce, Dolores. *Guido d'Arezzo's Regule Rithmice, Prologus in Antiphonarium, and Epistola ad Michahelem: A Critical Text and Translation, with an Introduction, Annotations, Indices, and New Manuscript Inventories*. Musicological Studies, vol. 73. Ottawa, 1999.

Sacks, Oliver. *Musicophilia: Tales of Music and the Brain*. New York, 2007.

Schleifer, Eliyahu. "Jewish Liturgical Music from the Bible to Hasidism." In *Sacred Sound and Social Change: Liturgical Music in Jewish and Christian Experience*, edited by Lawrence A. Hoffman. Notre Dame, Ind., 1992.

Smith, J. A. "The Ancient Synagogue, the Early Church and Singing." *Music and Letters* 65 (1984), pp. 1–16.

Stillman, Mimi. "The Music of Dante's *Purgatorio*." *Hortulus: The Online Graduate Journal of Medieval Studies* 1, no. 1 (2005), http://hortulus.net/journal/20052Stillman.pdf.

Strohm, Reinhard. *The Rise of European Music, 1380–1500*. Cambridge, 1993.

Subbioni, Marina. "Pittura e miniatura nei corali di San Domenico di Perugia." In *Canto e colore: I corali di San Domenico di Perugia nella Biblioteca comunale Augusta (XII–XIV sec.)*, edited by Claudia Parmeggiani. Exh. cat., Unicredit Banca, Perugia. Perugia, 2006.

Tacconi, Marica Susan. "Liturgy and Chant at the Cathedral of Florence: A Survey of the Pre-Tridentine Sources (Tenth–Sixteenth Centuries)." Ph.D. diss., Yale University, New Haven, 1999.
———. "The Maestro Daddesco and the Cathedral of Florence: A New Manuscript." *Burlington Magazine* 142, no. 1164 (March 2000), pp. 165–70.
———. "Appropriating the Instruments of Worship: The 1512 Medici Restoration and the Florentine Cathedral Choirbooks." *Renaissance Quarterly* 56 (Summer 2003), pp. 333–76.
———. *Cathedral and Civic Ritual in Late Medieval and Renaissance Florence: The Service Books of Santa Maria del Fiore*. Cambridge, 2005.

Vasari, Giorgio. *Le vite de' più eccellenti pittori, scultori ed architettori*. Notes and annotations by Gaetano Milanesi. Based on the 2d ed. of 1568. Florence, 1906.

Webster, Douglas Raymund. "The Carthusian Order." In *The Catholic Encyclopedia*, vol. 3. New York, 1908. Electronic edition: www.newadvent.org/cathen/03388a.htm.

Weissman, Ronald F. E. *Ritual Brotherhood in Renaissance Florence*. New York, 1982.

## Acknowledgments

I would like to thank Alison Manges Nogueira, Jonathan J. G. Alexander, Thomas Kren, Richard Porterfield, Peter Barnet, Nancy Wu, Margaret Lawson, Stuart W. Pyhrr, Keith Christiansen, Dirk H. Breiding, Dita Amory, Carmen C. Bambach, Asia Mernissi, Manon Six, Christine E. Brennan, Evelyn Cohen, Christine McDermott, Robert Theo Margelony, and Thomas P. Vinton, all of whom have at various stages assisted with this project. Research by Laurence B. Kanter and Pia Palladino on the illuminations from the collection of Robert Lehman has contributed significantly to the study of choral illuminations and forms an important background to this essay.

## Photograph Credits and Copyright Notices